LET'S START A PUPPET THEATRE

LET'S START A PUPPET THEATRE

BENNY E. ANDERSEN

 VAN NOSTRAND REINHOLD COMPANY
New York   Cincinnati   London   Toronto   Melbourne

This book was originally published in Danish under the title *Comediespil med dukker* by Høst & Søns Forlag, Copenhagen, Denmark. *Comediespil med dukker* copyright © Høst & Søns Forlag 1971

Translated from Danish by Hugh Young
English translation © Van Nostrand Reinhold Company Ltd., 1973

Drawings by Ole Bruun-Rasmussen
Photographs by Tove Parbst
Colour photograph on the cover by Jens Bull.
Library of Congress Catalog Card
Number: 73-3940
ISBN 0 442 29986 9

All rights reserved. No part of this work covered by the copyright hereon may be reproduced or used in any form or by any means—graphic, electronic, or mechanical, including photocopying, recording, taping, or information storage and retrieval systems— without written permission of the publisher.

This book is set in Bembo and is printed in Great Britain by Jolly & Barber Ltd., Rugby and bound by the Ferndale Book Company.

Published by Van Nostrand Reinhold Company, Inc., 450 West 33rd St., New York N.Y. 10001 and Van Nostrand Reinhold Company Ltd., 25-28 Buckingham Gate, London SW1E 6LQ.

Published simultaneously in Canada by Van Nostrand Reinhold Company Ltd.

Van Nostrand Reinhold Company Regional Offices: New York Cincinnati Chicago Millbrae Dallas.

Van Nostrand Reinhold Company International Offices: London Toronto Melbourne.

16 15 14 13 12 11 10 9 8 7 6 5 4 3 2 1

Contents

FOREWORD	7
THE PLAY	9
A shoe-play	9
Plays are all round us—and within us	10
A big tuft of raffia	10
THE STAGE	12
The thirsty doorhandle	12
The theatre stage	12
The short-sighted mop	13
LIGHTING	17
The projector	17
Shadows	18
Shadow play with a stick	18
Shadows in the window	18
Coloured lights	20
SOUND	22
The possibilities of sound with puppets	24
The tape-recorder	25
A sneeze-play	27
THE PUPPET	30
Bag puppets	32
The puppet, play	31
The actor is forgotten	32
The prima donna	32
THE PUPPET THEATRE	36
A hook and a blind-frame	36
The height of the theatre	36
Hanging up the frame	37
The proscenium	37
The stage	37
The back curtain	37
The theatre is ready	38
The curtain	38
Spotlights	39
Scenery	39
The prima donna's début	39
MORE PUPPETS	42
Rod puppets and glove puppets	42
Carved heads	42
Moulded heads	47
Bodies	50
Glove puppets	54
Other puppets	57
Hair and beard	61
Colours	63
The prima donna receives a visit	63
MORE THEATRES	67
The prima donna's theatre and the new puppet's theatre	67
Construction frames	68
An open theatre	69
The closed theatre	73
Bigger theatres	78
Other theatres	78
POSTSCRIPT	86
Some books about the puppet theatre	86
Warning	86
What shall we act?	86
WHERE DO YOU GET WHAT?	88
USEFUL TOOLS TO HAVE	91

A pretty couple. A love-story seen through the play actor's magic mirror? Or just two rod puppets, he with a huge glove-hand and she with a little hand like a back-scratcher. Both hands are fitted with action rods.

Foreword

Without very close collaboration with Ole Bruun-Rasmussen this book would never have been possible. He has given me a great many ideas which are incorporated in a large number of the book's practical instructions. His drawings are not just illustrations but independent contributions, and many of his puppets form the foundation for the book's little plays. Unless otherwise indicated, the puppets in the photographs in the book were all made by him.

In addition, a number of artists who work in the children's theatre 'Comedy Wagon' have put their puppets and their ideas at my disposal and Kirsten Ewaldsen and Ib Permin have made helpful comments on the text.

I thank them all for their help.

Benny E. Andersen

A table with partly made puppets and materials. We shall meet some of the materials immediately— for instance look what the lobster claw and the bottle-brush have become by the next picture. The loofah, the sock, the ostrich feather and the wire will reappear later.

The Play

In every human being, in every part of the human body, there is concealed a desire to act, to make a play. It is waiting only to break out from the restraints and inhibitions that hold it back. It is there in most small children; even adults, when they are in the mood, will indulge in a bit of clowning or a little play-making.

There is a play in the objects all around – clouds, trees, bushes become creatures of fantasy if the imagination is allowed free rein. Small children see them the whole time – shadows, secret corners, even spots and stains on a wall or bedroom ceiling, can become the creatures of their fantasy world.

A SHOE-PLAY

A play can make use of ordinary, everyday things, without having to adapt them specially. Throw a pair of men's shoes down on the floor. Hold them by the heels, and make them walk about. They're still only shoes, but they seem to take on a life of their own. They may walk off, weary and exhausted. Then they meet a pair of ladies' shoes. The ladies' shoes trip to one side. The men's shoes cheer up and walk after them. The ladies' shoes turn away. The men's shoes are persistent. The ladies' shoes get more interested. Contact is made. The toes of the shoes meet. Then the shoes go off 'arm in arm'.

So you think shoes can't go arm in arm? You try it. It works marvellously. They walk close together, he and she, two and two. And when it's all over they can go back to

PERFORMERS:
a pair of men's shoes
a pair of ladies' shoes
two actors

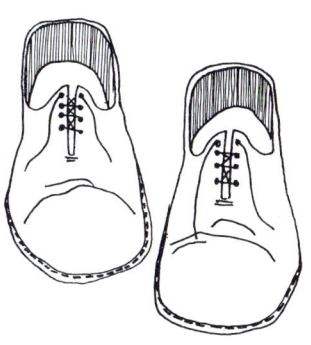

There is nothing in the world that cannot be made into a puppet play. It begins with tragedy and ends in comedy.

being ordinary shoes again. The plot can be varied in lots of ways: the shoes might not get on so well, or they might begin to quarrel.

A coat draped over a lobster claw or a bottle—it could be a witch.

PLAYS ARE ALL ROUND US – AND WITHIN US

The shoes were ordinary everyday objects, but we brought them to life. We used them as *puppets* and we put on a *puppet play*.

There are plays within us too, in our faces or our fingers. People who think they've never played with their fingers have just forgotten.

This book is mostly about play-acting with puppets, but we shouldn't forget the potential of our own bodies just because we're putting on puppet shows. A play makes use of whatever offers the best possibilities at the moment. We should use anything that's within reach. And as well as the puppets that includes ourselves!

PERFORMERS:
a big tuft of raffia
a hat
an umbrella
one actor

A BIG TUFT OF RAFFIA

We lay a big tuft of raffia on the floor. A puppet actor walks on. He spots the raffia and looks at it with astonishment. What on earth is it? He walks round it and approaches it

10

gingerly. He looks nervous but at the same time curious. With his face turned away, he pokes at the raffia with an outstretched finger. This makes the raffia move and the actor steps back nervously. He peeps back at the odd-looking tuft, now lying quite still.

A living raffia-animal

He tries various ways of approaching it, some friendly, some severe. He may caress it, kick it, cuff it and talk to it. Each time he makes it react with some movement. Next he plucks up courage and picks it up in his hand, where it takes on the look of a lively raffia-animal. He holds it close and strokes it. It may try to jump away from him, but he grabs it at the last moment.

Then he may try to put it on his head like a wig. But it keeps falling off. He gets cross, throws it down and ostentatiously turns his back on it. Feeling sorry for his unkindness he peeps surreptitiously over his shoulder at the raffia, which is lying quite still. Has it hurt itself? Is it dead? He leans over and strokes its fur. He picks it up again and caresses it. It starts to shiver, and he talks to it. It answers with a nod or a shake of the head.

Is it dead?

'Are you cold?'
'Would you like a hat on?'

He puts a hat on it and walks up and down with it. Then it shivers again.

'What's the matter now?'
'Are you afraid it's going to rain?'
'Do you want an umbrella?'

The actor asks one of the audience to put up the umbrella and hold it over the raffia-animal. Then he takes the umbrella with his free hand and he and the creature go out of the room together.

A tuft of raffia and an actor

A little play like that, with just one actor and one puppet, can have endless variations. The audience can take part, too. They can examine the tuft of raffia. They can stroke it. They can try it on like a wig. If they treat it as if it were alive then it *is* alive!

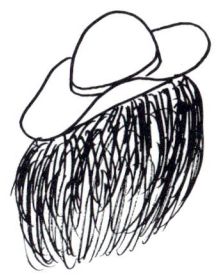

The raffia-animal wearing its hat.

The Stage

The kind of plays we have discussed so far can be varied and developed from a simple game to the virtuoso art of the theatre. The actor and his puppet can perform where they like among the audience, and it is a good idea to get the audience to take part.

PERFORMERS:
a mug with a handle
a doorhandle
a pair of spectacles
one actor

THE THIRSTY DOORHANDLE

A mug of beer stands on a table. A doorhandle (or a hammer) goes up to it, wriggling, nodding and hopping along the table. Small movements work best as a rule. It sniffs at the mug and walks round for a while. Then it sticks its snout into the mug and drinks. It dances away, satisfied. Its thirst is slaked.

Now the actor puts a pair of spectacles on the mug. The mug peers at the handle that has had the nerve to drink out of its head. When the handle realizes that it has been bothering a real puppet, it gets shy and runs away. The spectacles are taken off the mug, and the play is over.

The handle is moved quite openly with two fingers round the shaft. The actor uses his other hand to put the spectacles on the mug and take them off again. If he turns the mug from side to side with little jerks, he can make it look as if it is glaring with surprise and annoyance at the handle. As in the previous example, the audience can sit wherever they like.

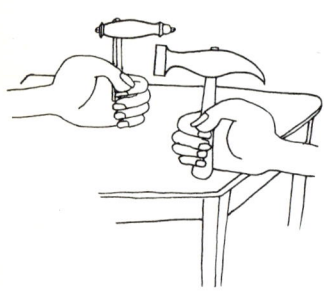

Here comes the hammer— hop hop hop—and here comes the doorhandle—bump bump bump.

Also a curious pair of spectacles.

THE STAGE

It is also possible to have the audience on one side of the table and the actor on the other. Now the actor can move the handle along the side of the table away from the audience. He keeps his hand hidden behind the edge of the table, heightening the illusion that the handle is really alive. It seems to move without help. Only the actor's hand is hidden, while the rest of him is taking part in the play – apparently having no connection with the handle.

With his free hand he puts the spectacles on the mug and moves it as before without hiding his hand. He thus has a visible connection with the mug, but none with the handle. This makes it look as if he is teasing the handle, making it believe that the mug is a living puppet like itself.

This little play within a play is one of the many new possibilities that arise when you introduce a stage – in this case, the side of the table.

The audience are on one side of the stage and the actors on the other, in front of the footlights. It's the way a lot of theatre business is carried on, and it makes it easy to keep the audience quiet. They sit as they would in front of a television screen, ready to be entertained. However, the stage needn't create such a dull situation; you can play on both sides of it and there are many ways of using it informally to develop the play's potential. That's why we welcome it.

What's he staring at me like that for?

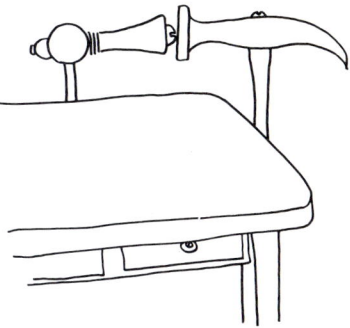

A love scene—a kiss.

THE SHORT-SIGHTED MOP

A table can be turned over on its side to make a simple puppet theatre. The upper edge of the table forms the stage that you act on. The actor hides behind the table. He can sit on a little stool or, better, on a little board with wheels (such as piano castors) screwed on so that they will turn.

PERFORMERS:
a floor mop without its handle.
On its 'nose' (which might be a dressmaker's hook) you can put
a lorgnette made out of wire
a book
a stick
a hat
if necessary a glove
one actor

A hook sewn on makes a good nose for the lorgnette.

13

The short-sighted mop with its lorgnette.

The lorgnette can be made of steel wire for example fencing wire.

A little vehicle for the puppet player can be made from a round board fitted with rotating piano-castors. A foam-rubber cushion is laid on it and covered with strong material, nailed down with carpet tacks.

The board can be padded with a cushion and its height must be such that the actor's head is not visible over the top of the table.

The audience sit in front of the table. On the floor in front of the table lie a book, a stick and a hat. The actor holds the mop with one hand. (This hand should be in the position it would be in to take a brush.) With his other hand, which may have a glove on it, he holds the lorgnette. This hand is not seen while it's controlling the lorgnette, but once the actor has put the lorgnette on the mop's nose, his free hand becomes the mop's hand which takes the book, hat and stick as the audience pass them to him.

THE PLAY BEGINS

The mop comes cautiously out from behind the stage. Only the top of it is visible. It disappears again as quick as a flash, then slowly comes up again. It repeats this several times until it is completely up. It coughs. Now the lorgnette comes up behind the mop. It says, 'Psst!' and the mop tries

14

to catch it. It chases the lorgnette all over the stage. But at the edge of the stage the lorgnette ducks down and disappears. Then it comes up on the opposite side (as far as the actor's arm can reach). The mop starts the chase again, but finally gives up and asks the audience to help.

We hope that someone in the audience is prepared to do so. The mop asks the helper to come up to the stage and sit on the floor in front of the table in such a way that he doesn't block the view of the rest of the audience. It asks him to hold the stick up in the air and to hold the handle up and move it about, so that it looks like an animal – a stick-animal. The head of the stick makes small, quick, controlled movements from side to side.

The mop then talks to the stick-animal, which can answer by nodding or shaking its head. (The mop must tell the helper about that too.)

'Hallo, little stick-animal.'

'Will you help me catch the glasses?'

'You must go up to them very carefully or they'll get frightened and run away. And then I can't see.'

The mop's beard is here behind the stage. The actor puts his gloved hand forward.

Thanks for your help!

The helper should then move the stick towards the lorgnette, which, threatened in this way, will jump up and sit on the mop's nose.

The actor now has one hand free. He puts it out on the stage, close to the mop so that it looks like the mop's own hand. It beckons the stick over and pats it on the head. Then the mop asks for the book. It holds the book upside down and begins to read in a funny sort of made-up language. The audience may notice that the book is upside down, or perhaps the mop will have to find it out itself. Either way, it bumbles on and does a little clowning.

'A book shouldn't stand on its head. Hats stand on heads.'

Perhaps it gets a laugh by laying the book on its head. Then it asks to have its hat put on, which is another job for the helper. And now the mop is ready to read the book – the right way up this time.

'I'll read you a poem. It's about you, little stick. Would you like to hear it?'

If the stick says 'Yes', it reads the poem. Otherwise the show ends here. When you're playing to an audience you always have to be prepared for the unexpected.

> *Little stick, down there below*
> *You're the nicest stick I know.*
> *Now we two have finished talking*
> *I can use you when I'm walking.*

With these words the mop grabs the stick from the helper. It thanks him for his help and strolls along the stage leaning on the stick. If necessary it repeats the poem.

Lighting

There's bound to be a certain amount of light wherever you are, and of course you can act a play without bothering much about the effect the light will have on what you're doing, just taking it for granted. But you will automatically turn out a harsh, ugly overhead light if it ruins the atmosphere. You will draw the blinds over the window if the sun gets in the eyes of the audience and you will also arrange yourself in the room so that the puppets and the actors will be seen to the best advantage. In short, consciously or unconsciously, you *do* work with the lighting.

THE PROJECTOR

Who hasn't at some time tried holding a torch under his face on a dark evening? Lit from below, the face looks odd and grotesque. Light used in that sort of way can be very effective with puppets. The puppet's face is of course always the same, but if its head is moved about in the light of the projector its face takes on the most varied expressions.

For projectors you can use the type of reading lamps found in drawing offices, which can be turned and adjusted in many ways. In the play about the short-sighted mop you can fix two of these lamps to the stage, arranging them so that the lights slants down on to the stage from either side.

1. If the puppet is lit from behind the light gets in the audience's eyes.
2. The puppet properly lit, so that it comes to life.
3. More lights may wipe out the puppet's features, so that it almost loses its shape and looks flat.

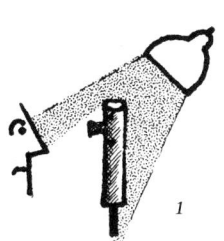
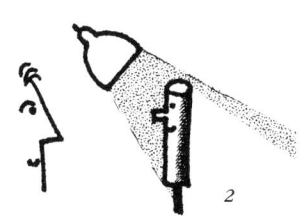

The best way to learn how to use lighting properly is by trial and error. If you are continually moving the puppets about under different lighting conditions you can't help noticing which effect looks best in a given situation.

SHADOWS

Stick-animal with shadow twin.

The light will often cast heavy shadows, but don't worry about that. It can make the puppets look wonderful, and anyway we are not dealing with a naturalistic world. Indeed the shadows may turn into extra actors.

For example, hold up a stick against a light background to make a stick-animal. Light it from in front with a reading lamp, and you have a shadow twin of the stick-animal. That's enough to make a play.

SHADOW PLAY WITH A STICK

PERFORMERS: *on actor*
a stage (a table on its side)
light background (light of a single colour)
a stick lit from in front by a reading lamp which must be the dominant source of light (preferably the only source)
a shadow stick also appears

The stick walks about the stage like a stick-animal. It is controlled by an actor hidden behind the stage. Suddenly it catches sight of its shadow on the wall. It tries to stop the shadow moving – the shadow stops too. The stick goes backwards – so does the shadow. The stick tries to catch the shadow, but without success, until at last the stick goes right up to the back-curtain and catches the shadow with a kiss.

SHADOWS IN THE WINDOW

The shadow play mentioned above is rather like the shadow plays you can make on a wall with your hands and fingers – something most people must have tried. But you can also make another kind of shadow play and use it as an item in a puppet show. Cut a house out of plywood with a saw, using four- or five-ply about $\frac{3}{16}$ in. (5 mm.) thick, or make it out of cardboard $\frac{1}{8}$ in. (3 mm.) thick. Cover the window with thin white fabric or tissue paper. Fix the house to the stage with a screw clip and light it from behind with a reading lamp. If the puppet – in this case the stick – stands behind the house, its shadow will fall on the window fabric. To the audience, it will seem to be standing inside the house. Only its shadow is visible on the drawn blind (the light from in front must not be too strong, or it will drown the shadow picture). But the stick can also walk out of the house and act like an ordinary puppet.

If the house is made of plywood there are further possibilities. You can fix a roller-blind, or a curtain on an ordinary curtain rod, to the back of the house. Once again you can play with the shadow effects when the curtain is drawn, but when you open it the audience will be able to see the puppet standing in the window quite clearly. (Remember to switch off the shadow play lamp or it will shine into the faces of the audience.)

Helle Ryslinge and Tom Nagel Rasmussen used this effect in their puppet play, 'Tony in the Whistling Marsh'. In the picture you can see Tony talking with his friend the owl through the open window. The window is cut more or less straight and the window frame is represented. There are two pieces of fabric sewn on as curtains. A blind is nailed above, with a round stick inserted into the hem of its bottom edge. When rolled up it is fastened with a bow,

One stick is out of doors and one in the house behind the rolled-down blind.

The blind is pulled up. 'Here I am,' says the stick. But now what's happened to the other one?

The owl tempts the boy out on a night adventure.

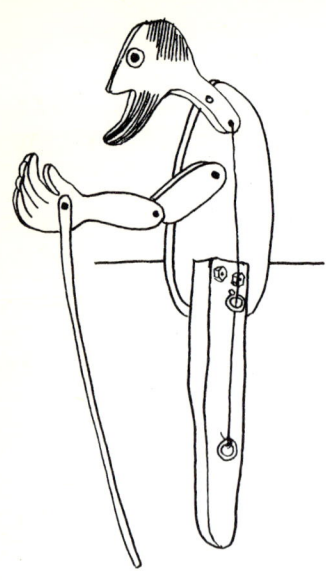

and when the two puppets have finished talking the bow is undone and the blind falls down. A light is switched on behind the blind and the owl is seen as a shadow, out in the moonlight.

REAL SHADOW-PUPPETS

We shall not deal here with real shadow plays, produced with shadow effects only. We will just mention that shadow puppets are usually flat. They can be of plywood or cardboard and are made so that they can move, as shown in the drawings. One way of making them is to cut them out of the colour filters used for stage lights; these filters can be bought in big sheets from shops that sell theatre equipment. If these coloured, transparent puppets are brought right up against the screen the effect can be very pretty.

The shadow puppet is operated by means of a handle attached to its body with two screws. The bearded man's arm is moved by means of a stick held with the other hand. He can nod too. A ring is tied to the end of the string so that it can be hooked on to a nail or screw.

The tail and the lower jaw of the shadow horse move up and down when the strings are pulled. If the lower jaw and tail tend to fall too low when the strings are released, the strings must be hooked on to a nail.

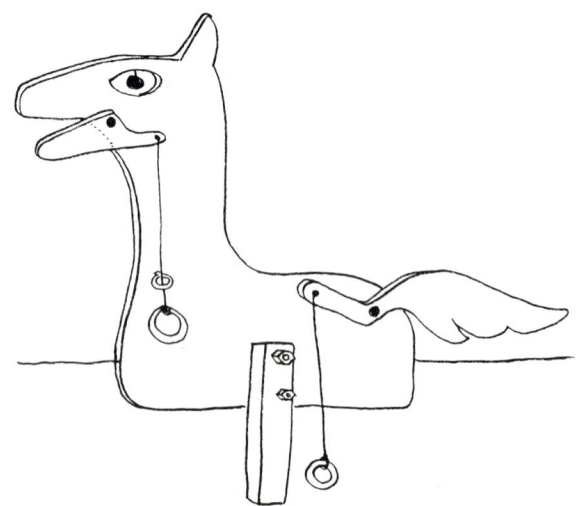

COLOURED LIGHTS

You can light the stage, the puppets and the actors from the front with coloured lights. The endless different shades of colour offer countless possibilities for using colour to create whatever atmosphere you need.

You can also buy colour filters to put in front of lamps from firms that deal in theatre equipment. These are made of a kind of strong, coloured plastic sheet which does not melt in the heat from the lamps. If you use reading lamps as projectors, you can cut the filters into squares to fit on the front of the lamps. The parallel sides should be only a little bit bigger than the diameter of the lampshade. The filters are then fixed on with adhesive tape.

You can also fit coloured bulbs in the lamps. But as soon as you try to get a light shade (in other words, when the colours get stronger), the bulbs we work with here (maximum 60 watts) give a very weak light. The effect is therefore best used close up to the scenery, even actually in the wings, and in conjunction with white light from the front. If the light isn't strong enough, stronger lamps must be used (photographic lamps, proper projectors etc.).

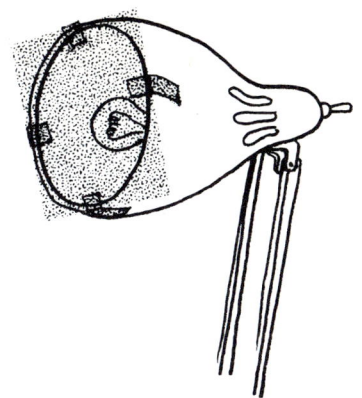
Lamp with colour filter.

There are several factors to take into account in using coloured lights. For example, figures and scenery have their own colours and these will be mixed with the coloured lighting. If you put a blue light on a yellow puppet, the puppet turns green, which can come as a surprise if you weren't expecting it.

Here are a few suggestions about coloured lighting. But, as we said before, we're not in a naturalistic world; the puppets have their own life, just as the play has, and you can easily think up new possibilities while you're actually working. Still, to give some examples of what's often done and can be done effectively, you can make:

twilight with yellow light
sunrise with red and yellow filters
sea and cold with light blue filters
forest effects with green and blue filters together
indoor scenes with yellow filter and dimmer light
(you can dim the light by using few, or weaker, bulbs; you can also use a variable resistance, which can be bought from firms that deal in physics equipment for schools).

It is generally agreed that the red/orange/yellow range of the spectrum gives an effect of warmth and the green/violet/blue one an effect of cold.

Sound

It is possible to do a play without sound, even if it is hard to be silent, but as a rule sound is a component part of the play and is just as important as what is seen.

You speak. You can speak lines written in advance and learnt by heart, or you may improvise on the basis of a skeleton script. But there is more to sound than speech. It also includes, for instance, the music and sound effects accompanying the play.

It can be very inspiring to turn on the gramophone and make up a little play to the music, possibly with no speech at all. You can also create background sounds and music with simple instruments like the rattles, toy trumpets, whistles and other noisy gadgets you get on such occasions as Christmas parties. All kinds of instruments are suitable: tom-toms, cymbals, triangle, xylophone, glockenspiel, tambourine, wood-blocks, castanets, maraccas, recorders, piano, guitar – there is hardly anything that can't be used.

With a kazoo you can make animal noises. The kazoo doesn't interfere with the operation of the puppet as both your hands are free. You can also buy a mouth-organ frame in a music shop. You can hang it round your neck and fit the kazoo into it.

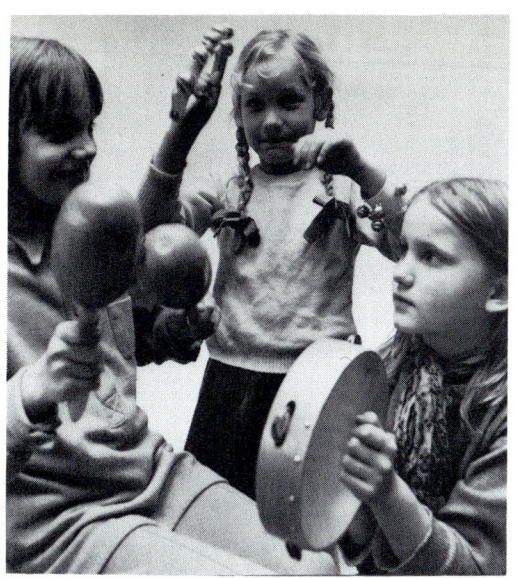
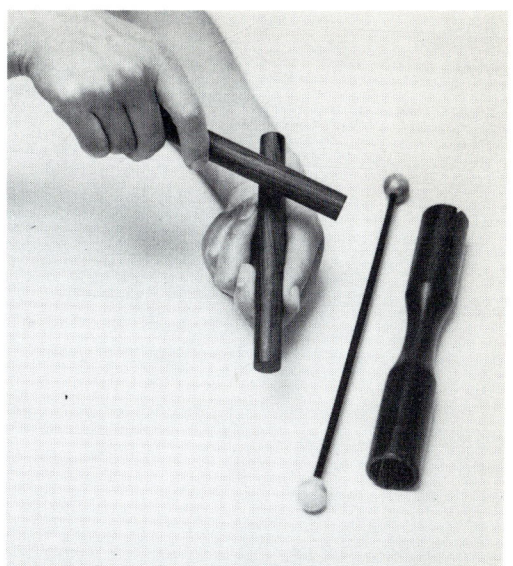

Top left, maraccas, bells and tambourine. In the next picture you can see, on the left, two solid pieces of wood and, on the right, a hollow piece, which gives different sounds when you hit one end or the other with the drumstick, also seen in the picture. Below left, glockenspiel, cymbals and bongos (hand drums); in front, pan pipes. Bottom right, a melodica. There are different makes of melodica. The model shown here is obtainable in soprano (green) and alto (red); the latter has a nicer tone.

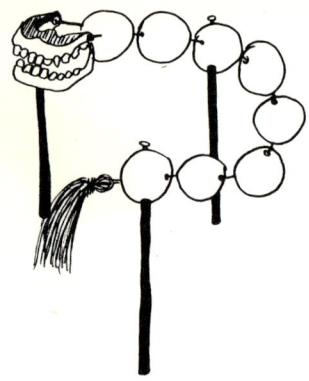

It isn't necessary to give a performance in the grand manner on your instrument. Most people can manage a simple rhythm, and with just a few notes you can emphasize what's happening on the stage.

Special mention must be made of the kazoo, that modern version of the comb and tissue paper. You can keep it in your mouth while you operate the puppets and just sing into it or make whatever noises you want the puppets to produce if they don't use ordinary speech. Try for instance making the tuft of raffia in the play on page 12 give frightened squeaks on the kazoo whenever you touch it.

The false teeth came from a police auction of lost property, but you can get false teeth made of plastic in joke shops. The table tennis balls are threaded on string like beads, the tassel can be made of coloured raffia. The tooth-snake is controlled by rods.

THE POSSIBILITIES OF SOUND WITH PUPPETS

Sound and music can often replace speech in a play and most puppets suggest possibilities of sound that are well worth working out.

A hand stuffed into a knitted sock becomes a highly expressive sock-animal. Make the animal move to the accompaniment of different sounds and see which ones suit it best.

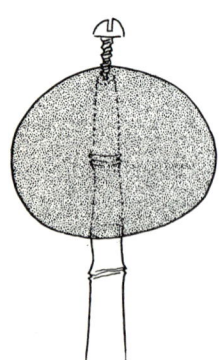

To put the table tennis balls on rods use hollow sticks (bamboo) and screw them down with screws which fit into the hollow part. The false teeth are fixed in the same way.

The sock-animal bows low before an ostrich feather, which must be at least a duchess.

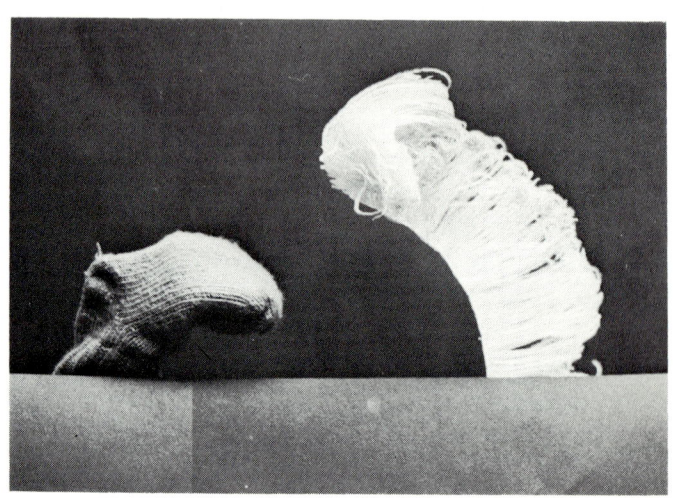

It is possible to make a fine puppet out of a set of false teeth and a string of pingpong balls: a tooth-snake. What sort of noise goes with this? Maraccas? Nails in a tin? Tambourine? Whatever it is, it certainly won't be the same as the noise that fitted the sock-animal.

The pictures show some puppets and children with instruments. Children and grown-ups agreed that the triangle suited the fish, recorders the birds, and castanets the pretty lady with the large bosom and great big eyes.

Tingaling! Triangle and fish. Tweet tweet! Birds' voices are deep, since it is a big flute (also recorder). A smaller flute gives higher sounds.

THE TAPE RECORDER

With the aid of a tape recorder you can record and play back anything from simple sound effects to orchestral music. You can even record a whole puppet play on tape and play it back so that the puppets simply have to follow the text and music. The actors do not have to speak themselves, and are therefore called puppet manipulators. You can also make puppets and people act together, so that the puppets speak from a tape and the people use their own voices.

When a tape recorder is used in this way it is most effective if the speaker is placed close to the puppets.

Most of the tapes used for professional puppet shows are

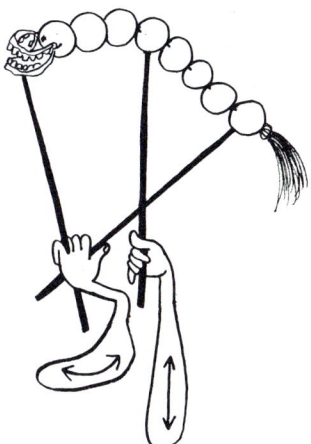

A puppet actor can work a tooth-snake as shown in the picture. The arms must move simultaneously. For the use of action rods see page 51.

25

A fiery rhythm on the castanets, but both music and dance need practice.

recorded in soundproof studios with very expensive apparatus, and if you hadn't realized that, you may well be disappointed by the quality of the sound that can be produced at home using an ordinary tape recorder in an ordinary room. However, you don't need an expensive tape recorder to play professionally made tapes.★

CUTTING TAPES

You generally find you have to cut the tapes. You cannot do this with ordinary scissors, which are magnetic and make a click in the recording, nor can you join the tape with ordinary tape, which will get broken. However, you can buy special non-magnetic scissors and special tape for these operations in the bigger radio shops. You can also get white and coloured tapes, which are very handy when the recorder has to be stopped during the performance as they help show where to stop and where to start up again.

And of course you will have to experiment. There are as a rule two sound-heads on a tape recorder. The one furthest to the right is the playing-head. It is there that you have to cut the tape when you have listened to the tape up to the point where something has to be cut out.

DISADVANTAGES OF TAPE RECORDERS

The tape recorder opens up many exciting possibilities for a puppet show, but the play can of course easily get inflexible if you depend too much on the sequence in which the sounds come. For this reason, and also because it's so difficult to make recordings of a satisfactory standard (professional studios are very expensive) you may often prefer to manage the sound without the use of tape.

★ When commercially recorded material is used for public performances of puppet shows a licence should be obtained from Phonographic Performance Ltd, 62 Oxford St., London W1N 0AN.

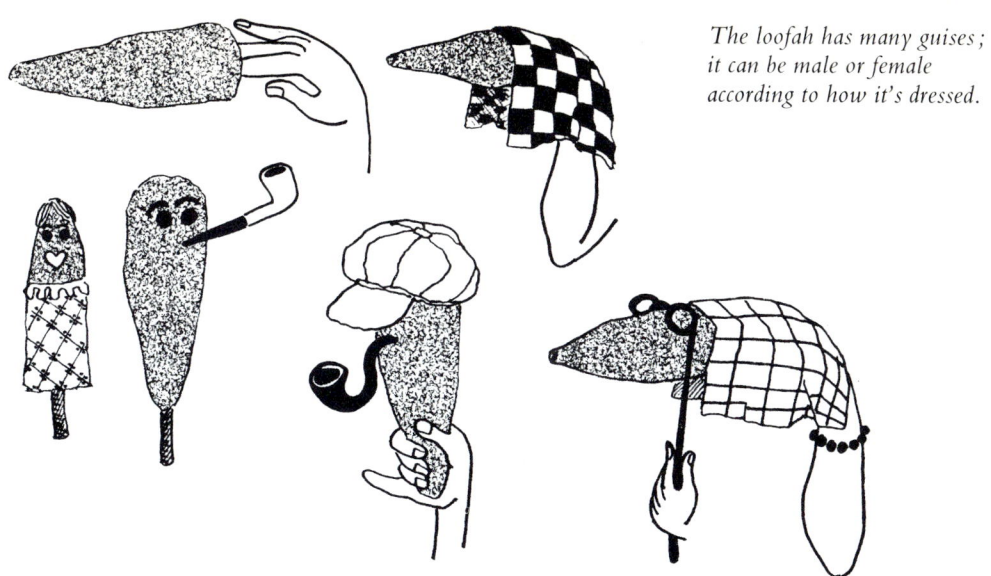

The loofah has many guises; it can be male or female according to how it's dressed.

A SNEEZE-PLAY

The toothache-animal consists of a loofah, which can be bought at a chemist's, with two fingers in a couple of holes and a towel over them. Why is it called a toothache-animal? I can't imagine, but some children christened it and thereby created another of those mysteries typical of the theatre: a toothache-animal that makes people sneeze. Isn't that clear?

For the theatre we can once again use a table laid on its side or we can make use of one or two boards with rugs over them. One actor (call him A) sits behind the stage so that the audience can't see him. He operates the toothache-animal for part of the time, and the mop for the rest. He must have a kazoo in his mouth or in a mouth-organ frame.

In front of the table there is another actor (call him B) who operates the toothache-animal part of the time and for the rest plays on or more instruments.

If more light is needed on the stage, it can be provided by two reading lamps, one on each side. However, you must have the rest of the room lit or you won't see either B or the audience he is sitting among. An ordinary ceiling light will do, or daylight (draw a curtain if it's too bright).

PERFORMERS:
the toothache-animal
a floor-mop
one actor behind the stage, with kazoo
one actor in front of the stage with another musical instrument
a table with a side (wooden boxes with a rug)

27

THE PLAY BEGINS

B stands or sits in front of the stage. He plays an instrument – a little tune or just a few notes. It doesn't matter if he sounds as if he's only practising.

Suddenly he sneezes. He plays and sneezes alternately. Then he goes round and looks among the audience.

'The toothache-animal must be somewhere here,' he says.

'I always sneeze when it comes near me. It's a dear little animal with a long snout and a towel on its head.'

He goes on playing and sneezing. The toothache-animal bobs up from behind the stage, in time with the music. Each time it comes up B sneezes. It's only when it begins to join in with the music with kazoo-talk that B notices it.

'Hallo, toothache-animal,' he says. 'A-choo!'

The toothache-animal talks with the kazoo.

'I always sneeze when you come. A-choo!'

Kazoo-talk.

B sings and the toothache-animal kazoos the following little song (only two or three notes in the tune):

A-choo! A-choo!
I've got the flu.

A mop and a loofah in friendly conversation. The eyes and spectacles on the mop and the loofah's nose are made from egg-trays (from the puppet play 'The Golden Toad').

Perhaps the audience can be persuaded to sneeze too.

'We must get hold of the mop,' says B. 'It can sweep the sneeze germs right away.' He sings again:

> *A-choo! A-choo!*
> *I've got the flu.*
> *Mop, mop,*
> *Make it stop.*

'Can you see the mop over where you are?' B asks the toothache-animal.

The toothache-animal says no with the kazoo and shakes its head.

'Come over here and let's look together,' says B.

B takes over the toothache-animal from A and takes it in his hand. Then they go round the room sneezing, searching for the mop and asking everyone!

'Have you seen the mop? Have *you*? Have *you*?'

The toothache-animal puts its snout in people's pockets and sniffs all round.

After searching vainly for some time B says:

'Perhaps we can play hunt-the-mop, and you tell us whether we're getting hot or cold.'

He tells the audience to say a-choo if they see the mop and to sneeze louder the nearer he gets to the mop.

The game begins. The mop keeps bobbing up first in one place, then in another. B and the toothache-animal search and the audience sneeze loudly when they get near the mop and more softly when they get further away from it. At last they find what they're looking for, and the sneezing stops. A holds the mop in one hand and takes the toothache-animal with the other. B takes up his instrument again and sings, with A joining in on the kazoo:

> *Bless you, bless you, dear old mop,*
> *Now you've made my sneezing stop.*

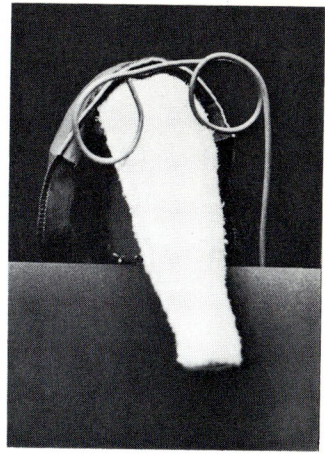

The spectacles seem to be a bit too big!

29

The Puppet

Anything that takes your fancy can be used as a puppet. An object may be sufficient in itself, or you may like to fit it out with spectacles, eyes, mouth, clothes, hat and so on. That's how all the puppets we've dealt with so far began.

But you may want to make a puppet from the very beginning. It may have to be used in some particular connection so that old shoes, mops, umbrellas and that sort of thing are no good.

So let's create a puppet that is all your own work and becomes an independent being, one that you can never let go of, because it has become like your own child. Think of the story of Pinocchio. It's all about a puppet that finally turns into a child – the old puppet-maker's own flesh-and-blood child.

Fringe beard and king's crown, button eyes, nose and mouth cut out of cloth are all sewn on to a velvet bag.

BAG PUPPETS

Bag puppets are very easy to make. You can just sew a long cloth bag together and embroider a face on it. Such things as scraps of cloth, beads and buttons can be sewn on for eyes, nose and mouth. The bag can be either a head or a whole body, with or without arms.

Now pull the bag on to your arm. If the bag makes the puppet's whole body, it's best to make it long enough to reach to your elbow. That makes it easier to move about and it is supported when you rest your elbow on a table, a knee, another arm, a ledge or whatever. It doesn't hover in the air.

The puppet can follow the movements of your hand and how the fingers should be placed will differ from one puppet to another and from one person to another. You have to keep trying until you find the most relaxed position for your hand. There's quite enough strain on your muscles in daily life and there's no reason to increase it with puppetry.

THE PUPPET PLAY

To start with try to use the puppet without any outside help, as that's a good way to get to know it. You can act by yourself or in front of an audience, just resting it on a table, knee, arm or stage and talking to it.

You can use ventriloquism, with the puppet doing the talking. You can also alter your voice just a little. The puppet can answer questions by nodding or shaking its head, or it can whisper things in the actor's ear. It's important to

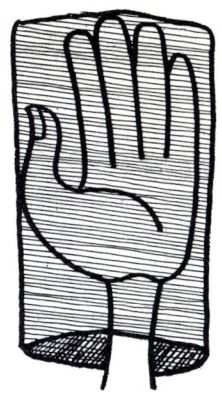

This is how the king's head in the photograph looks if we draw a plan of it. If the puppet is also to have a body, the bag will have to go right up to the elbow.

If you cut out the bag with three flaps to fit your fingers, you have the basis for a more sophisticated puppet. It has now got arms and can therefore pick things up, wave its hands and so on.

move the puppet every time it speaks, or reacts to what the actor says, and to keep it still the rest of the time.

Movements must be appropriate to what is being said. If you flap the puppet around too much the movement ceases to be effective. Small movements and pauses in between work very well because then you've got more in reserve when you want to express excitement, anger, happiness and so on.

THE ACTOR IS FORGOTTEN

The actor can make the puppet take over the whole show. It can talk with his normal voice, while he just looks on as the audience do; he's swallowed up by the puppet and after a while nobody notices him.

It's essential for him to concentrate completely on the puppet and this isn't usually difficult, particularly if it is a glamorous creation: perhaps a beautiful prima donna?

PERFORMERS:
a puppet prima donna
the tuft of raffia
the mop
the toothache-animal
shoes
doorhandle
mug with spectacles
other odds and ends used as puppets
table on its side
one or more boxes with rugs over them
two actors

THE PRIMA DONNA

An actor has made a pretty lady puppet (a bag puppet) and he lets it hang loosely with its head down. He does not put his hand in the bag, but just holds it with two fingers. He plays for a while with the dead puppet; he lifts its head, which drops back again limply when he lets it go; he looks into the bag; he puts his hand up and softly pulls the puppet by the arm. It's still dead, but now he makes it wake up slowly. He gradually makes the different parts of the puppet move. When it's wide awake he plays with it, making it jump and dance about.

'That's my puppet,' he says. 'I made it myself. Now it's waking up.'

The prima donna wakes up and stretches.

Interest is concentrated on the puppet. It's the puppet that talks, while the actor keeps in the background and is taken over by the puppet. He doesn't have to be a ventriloquist (see previous page).

The second actor comes up to the puppet. He shakes hands with it.

'Hallo, who are you?'
'I'm the puppet.'
'Which puppet?'
'Just the puppet, that's me.'
'We've got lots of puppets.'
'You can't have!'
'Yes, look here.'

The actor picks up a basket or a bag. It's full of odds and ends used as puppets – the mop, the tuft of raffia, shoes, doorhandle, mug with glasses and so on. He shows these to the new puppet one after another. He makes them look very lifelike, but the new puppet rejects them all, as in the following example:

'Look, these are some of our favourite puppets.' (The men's and ladies' shoes.) 'They go for a walk together.'
'Pooh! They're nothing but a lot of old shoes.'
'Well, then, look.' (He holds up the tuft of raffia.)
'An old hank of raffia. Pah!'

Gradually the puppet gets more and more superior and the actor more and more irritated. At last the actor says,

'Well, what do you think you are, anyway? A bag that someone's been sewing buttons on. Is that so much better?'
'Obviously. I'm an original work of art. Like a sculpture or a painting. There are piles of shoes and loads of raffia. But there's only one me. So there!'
'If you're so great, you ought to go on the stage.'
'Yes, and about time too. I'm just about fed up with hanging around here in these unsuitable conditions.'

The actor uses a table lying on its side as a theatre. He takes the mop and plays with it a bit. Then the mop calls over to the puppet,

'Hi, new puppet. Come over here and play with our puppet theatre. A prima donna's just what we need.'
'I will *not*. That's not a theatre. It's just an overturned table.'

Now the actor tries with a curtain over one or two boards or chairs. But the puppet turns them down too. It wants to have a proper theatre to act in. So it says:

'A proper theatre ought to have spotlights, to show how beautiful I am.'

'We've got a few reading lamps. What about those?'

'No good.'

Then the actor gets cross. He goes over and takes the puppet from the first actor's hand. He lets it dangle down loosely and says,

'I believe you're altogether too pleased with this puppet you've made. It's become a real conceited prima donna. It's unbearable. Can't you make its nose crooked, or do something else to make it ugly?'

'You must be crazy,' says the maker of the puppet. 'What would you say if I made your nose crooked? That's the way it's made and we must put up with it as it is. But let's make a puppet theatre for it.'

'All right, let's. But I don't believe that'll satisfy it.'

The actors pack up. And the next chapter tells how to build a little puppet theatre for the prima donna.

The Puppet Theatre

A HOOK AND A BLIND-FRAME

A single hook in the wall holds up the whole theatre, so it must be very firm. But before screwing it in we have to find out how high the theatre must hang.

The top side of the theatre is a blind-frame without cloth, such as is used for paintings; it can be bought in shops selling artists' materials. A handy size is 2 ft. 6 in. × 3 ft. (75 × 90 cm.). Take it apart first and reinforce the corner joints with glue; the little wooden wedges in the corners serve no purpose here and you can take them out.

You can also make a frame yourself. It must be very strong and the corners must be reinforced by screwing on angle-brackets.

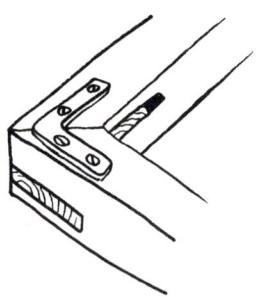

The corners of the frame must be secured with an angle bracket screwed on, or

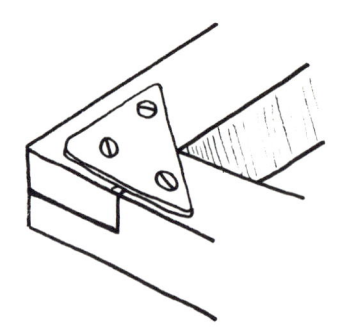

—with a triangular piece screwed on.

THE HEIGHT OF THE THEATRE

The theatre's height is determined by the height of the actors and by whether they perform sitting down or standing up. You can sit on a chair or a stool. If you like you can fit strong, revolving wheels (piano castors) on to a wooden box (a beer crate, for instance). You can also get chairs with wheels. This gives great mobility (see page 16). You measure from the floor to the top of the tallest actor's hair (sitting or standing) and then add about 2 ft. 3 in. (70 cm.). That gives you the height of the theatre.

The stage should ideally be just above the top of the actor's hair, so that he needn't be stooping and cramped, with his head bowed and so on, this can be a great strain on the muscles.

HANGING UP THE FRAME

Now we can screw the hook into the wall about 1 ft. 9 in. (50 cm.) above the level at which the top of the theatre is to hang. Fix four strings to the corners of the frame and cut them so that the frame hangs horizontally when the ends of the strings are tied together to a ring hanging on the hook.

THE PROSCENIUM

The theatre is made of cloth nailed to the frame. Here we only mention the front and back curtains which will be 3 ft. (90 cm.) wide. However, you can of course put up side curtains in the same way.

The front curtain is cut in one piece. The opening is about 4 in. (10 cm.) from the top and sides and about 2 ft. (60 cm.) high. You can prevent fraying with the help of glue, Bostik or Uhu for example. First glue where you have to cut; then let it dry and cut where it has been glued. If you want to edge the opening with zig-zag hems or frills you must allow about ¾ in. (2 cm.) for the seams.

This curtain is called the *proscenium*.

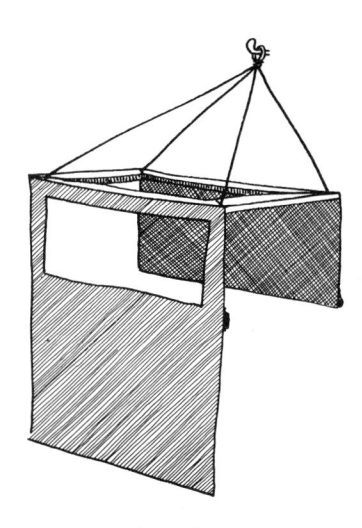

It's as simple as that! A blind-frame, a proscenium and a back curtain.

THE STAGE

Under the opening you sew a narrow hem of material forming a channel which is sewn to the back of the material. Instead of material you can use the kind of hessian used for chairs or sofas (you can get it from a craft materials supplier or saddler). Into the channel you fit a broad, flat batten. And there's your stage.

THE BACK CURTAIN

The back curtain is smaller but the bottom of it must not be visible when you look in through the opening. It might be about 3 ft. × 2 ft. 9 in. (90 × 80 cm.) if the theatre is the size suggested so far. A hem at the bottom into which a round stick is inserted gives weight to hold it in place.

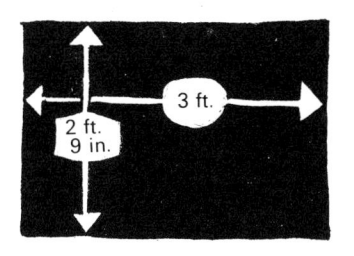

Measurements of the back curtain.

THE THEATRE IS READY

Fasten the curtains to the front and back sides of the blind frame, using small nails with large heads.

The theatre is now ready for you to sit down in it – or stand, if it's high enough.

Take the puppet in your hand and reach up into the air. Make sure the puppet doesn't lean backwards; in fact you will have to bend your wrists forward more than you probably expect. Let people on the other side check that the puppet looks natural when it moves on the stage. . . . But what's missing? Yes, a curtain!

THE CURTAIN

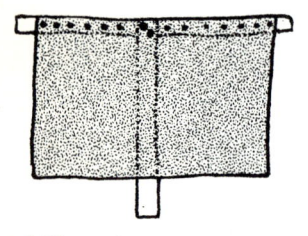

The curtain is quite simple to make. A piece of material, a little larger than the stage-opening, is nailed to a batten. The batten is a little longer than the width of the puppet theatre, so that it can lie on top of it. When the play begins, you just go out quite openly and take off the batten with the curtain. If you fit an extra batten at right angles so that the curtain rests on a T, you can sit inside the theatre and wriggle the curtain down.

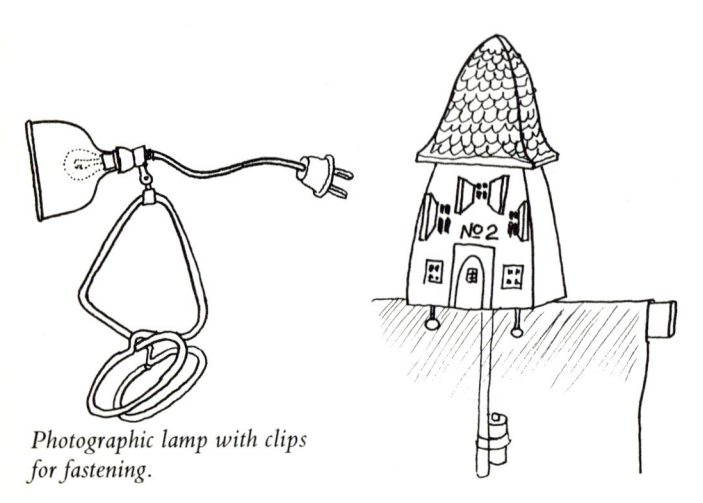

A T-curtain.

Photographic lamp with clips for fastening.

You can put scenery on to the ramp. This house (which incidentally is a space rocket from 'Prip and Prop', see p. 56) is fitted with a rod. It is made like a simple rod-puppet (see p. 52) and the rod is behind the proscenium curtain. If the house tips up, you can tie a counterweight on to it; a battery is used here. Two screws go down in front of the curtain and hold the weight in place. This kind of scenery can be brought on and taken off very quickly.

SPOTLIGHTS

A photographic lamp fixed on a table or a chair can work as a spotlight. You can get small frames for photographic lamps so that they can be clipped on to one side of the theatre. Reading lamps can of course also be used – so long as it doesn't upset the prima donna.

SCENERY

We can fit the blind-frame theatre with side curtains as described at the beginning of the instructions. And we can hang up scenery in the same way as we hang the curtain; it can be arranged in a number of ways. But if it gets too complicated it can easily become overloaded. It would then be better to build a theatre that stands on the floor, but we'll leave that till later (see page 67). Now we shall introduce the prima donna to her first theatre, hoping that it will satisfy her – for a time, anyway.

THE PRIMA DONNA'S DEBUT

PERFORMERS:
the new puppet theatre with a photographic lamp as a spotlight
musical instruments
the prima donna puppet and its maker (one actor)
one other actor

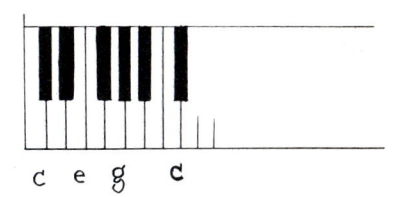

The curtain is down. The spotlight shines straight in on to the back curtain. The prima donna's creator is inside the theatre manipulating his puppet. The other actor is in front of the theatre, where he chats with the puppet and plays one or more musical instruments.

OVERTURE

There is a roll on the drum, a fanfare or other ceremonial music. A fanfare can be played on the notes C-E-G-C-G-E-C – the chord of C major. You can also shake a tambourine or do anything else you like, for instance, play the piano, recorder, xylophone or kazoo.

ACT I

Curtain up. (Down, actually.) The puppet is standing in the spotlight in the middle of the stage. It bows to all sides, while the fanfare continues. The actor in front of the stage stops the music and speaks to the puppet:

'Well, little prima donna. Is it a good theatre to act in?'

'Not so bad. I like having a curtain that goes up when the play begins. It creates a nice solemn atmosphere. It emphasizes my great acting skill and my beauty. But I wish you'd turn off that light that's shining straight in my eyes. I can't see a thing. It's really very tiresome.'

'You'll have to get used to that, little prima donna. That's what's it's like when you act in a grand theatre. It's all part of it. And you look very pretty in that lighting.'

'Well, that's a comfort. But I can't see you. You're absolutely in the dark.'

'You're not meant to see us. We have to see you. You're on display. What sort of act can you so?'

'Can't I just stand here and look pretty?'

'No. You've got to entertain us. Show us what you can do. Can you recite a poem?'

ACT 2

'Roses are red,
Violets are blue,
Strawberries are sweet
And I'm sweet too.'

'I don't think much of that. Can't you sing a song?'

'I will sing a little song
And it isn't very long,
Makedulla-makedilla-makeday.'

'No, well, that wasn't particularly long. Now you must try and make something up. When will you begin?'

'Begin? I've finished singing.'

'Is that all you can do? Do a little act. This is going to be an absolute flop.'

'Well, I can't think of anything.'

'Something funny, exciting, thrilling, or impressive . . .'

ACT 3

'Can't some of the other puppets help me?'

'There aren't any other puppets besides you.'

'Yes, there are. You showed me some.'

'Oh, those. Just old shoes and things like that. There's no place for them in that grand theatre.'

'They might help me to amuse the audience.'

'No, we'd better make some more puppets like you. Then you won't get conceited.'

'Is that necessary? Can't we get the audience to join in? Then I can still be the one and only prima donna.'

'I don't think we can expect too much from the audience when they're sitting there in the dark and looking up at this fine stage. We'd much better get busy making you some colleagues.'

FINALE

The curtain goes down to more fanfares. The prima donna bows to all sides.

More Puppets

ROD PUPPETS AND GLOVE PUPPETS

The prima donna may most accurately be described as a *glove puppet* or hand puppet, like Mr Punch in Britain, Mester Jakel in Denmark and Kasper in Germany. She is made out of a cloth bag, forming both head and body.

Glove puppets' heads and bodies are generally made separately, and this is also true of *rod puppets*.

The difference between glove puppets and rod puppets lies, not in their heads, which can be made in the same way, but in their bodies. The glove puppet's body is a glove drawn on to your hand and arm, while the rod puppet's body is a rod.

The heads can be made out of such things as cloth bags, rags, wood or papier mâché. Here we suggest and advise on two methods which produce light and very strong puppet's heads.

A puppet which is a combination of glove puppet and rod puppet. The hands are controlled by means of action rods as with rod puppets, but the body is a glove that fits over your hand and arm. The puppet has a club in one hand.

CARVED HEADS

ROD PUPPETS

You need expanded polystyrene, gauze (or tissue paper), wallpaper paste, synthetic resin (*not* cellulose-based) glue, plastic paints and sticks about 2 ft. 3 in. (70 cm.) long. (See the list of materials at the back of the book.)

The puppet's head is carved from the polystyrene/styrafoam. You can cut it with a hacksaw blade, without the saw, and a sharp knife.

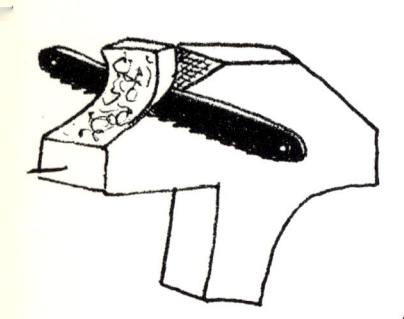

A hacksaw blade is good for polystyrene.

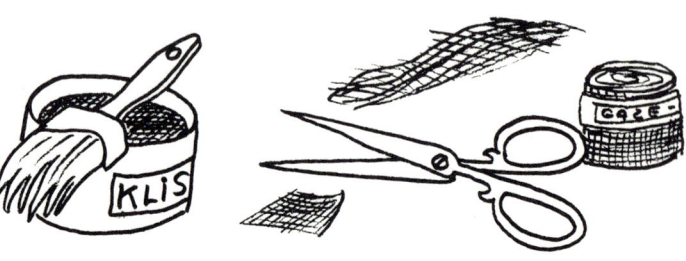

42

Sawing is a noisy business, and unfortunately it produces a lot of tiny plastic fragments which pick up an electric charge and stick to everything.

Cut a stick flat at one end and bore it into the neck from below. Remove it and put a little glue into the hole; then put the stick back and let the glue dry. Next cut the gauze into small pieces about the size of large postage stamps. Smear paste over the head and the upper part of the stick. Using the wet paste-brush, lay the pieces of gauze one by one on the head and smooth them down. Don't be mean with the paste. At least three layers of gauze must be applied, and it takes a long time. If you want a smoother surface you can stick bits of tissue paper on top in the same way.

The puppet now consists of a head on a stick. The head can be painted with plastic paints, and the rod puppet is basically complete.

A certain boldness of shape and colour goes well on the stage.

GLOVE PUPPETS

The same materials are used as for making the rod puppets' heads, but a short, thin stick or a roll of cardboard (from a toilet or kitchen roll) and some linen tape are also needed.

A glove puppet's head can be made exactly the same as a rod puppet's. The stick must be short and thin and can be held between the first and second fingers.

Normally, however, glove puppets are manipulated by one or more fingers inserted into a hole in the puppet's neck. In this case instead of inserting a stick into the carved polystyrene head, a cardboard roll is used and glued firmly in position.

First bore out the neck hole with the point of a stick of the same thickness as the cardboard roll, which can be made from an empty toilet roll or kitchen roll. You cut it lengthwise and stick it together again with glue and tape to whatever thickness you need, depending on the size of the finger or fingers with which you will control the head.

The cardboard roll should stick out about $1\frac{1}{4}$ in. (3 cm.) from the head and be the same thickness as the neck.

The place where the head and the neck meet and the cardboard neck itself should be covered with glue and gauze (or tissue paper) in the same way as the rest of the head.

A glove puppet's head fitted with a stick can be worked in this way. It enables the hand to be moved without the body moving too.

You can work glove puppets in a number of ways. Try your hand in the positions shown and choose the one that feels most relaxed and comfortable.

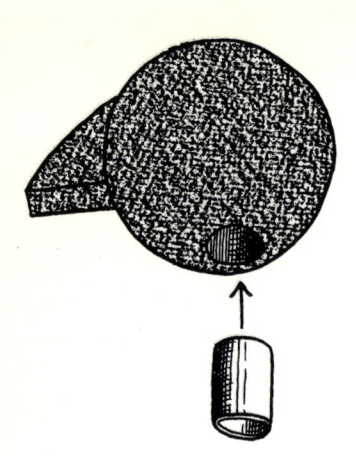

It's easier to attach the puppet's glove to the head if you put a collar at the bottom of the neck (i.e. cardboard roll) for the clothes to hang from. There are several ways of making this collar. For example, you can roll up a sausage of gauze and soak it in glue, then stick it to the roll and cover it with plenty of layers of gauze.

The drawings on this page show, above, a cardboard roll in position with the collar made of a narrow strip of paper rolled round the end of the roll. The whole of this is then covered with gauze.

Below, a cardboard roll with the collar made of string, tied tightly and fixed with glue. When the glue is dry the ends of the string can be cut off close to the knot. The whole of this is then covered with gauze.

When the neck-hold has been bored with a pointed stick the cardboard roll is put in.

PIECES OF EXPANDED POLYSTYRENE/STYRAFOAM GLUED TOGETHER

It may be difficult to work out what the head will look like when you just have a great block of expanded polystyrene which you must carve into a puppet's features. But you can also glue the head together from smaller pieces of polystyrene. It's much easier to carve a fine nose and glue it on to the puppet's head than to carve the whole head in one piece.

Use synthetic resin glue (not cellulose-based) and fix the two glued pieces together with pins, stuck right in up to the head. They can be left there after you have finished. Then you put on gauze and paste as before.

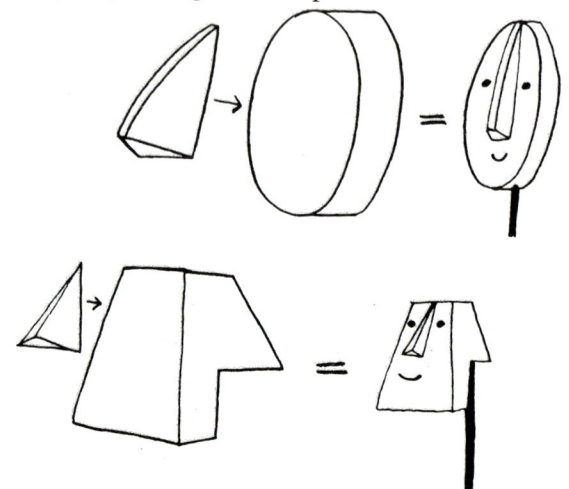

A roll of gauze is glued to the neck. It becomes a collar to which the glove can easily be attached.

Both heads and noses can be made in simple geometrical shapes.

It is easier to glue small and large pieces together than to cut the whole thing out.

MOULDED HEADS

GLOVE PUPPETS

Materials: modelling wax, vaseline, gauze (or tissue paper), synthetic resin glue (not cellulose), linen, carpet-thread. (See the list of materials at the back of the book.)

The head is shaped out of modelling wax (plasticine) which is very expensive, but can be used again for more heads. Crude, simple features are easiest to make since small, fine details easily disappear when the gauze is put on. The puppet's head must have a neck with a collar to make it easy to put on the puppet's clothes.

When the head is fully shaped you cut it lengthways into two halves. The halves are put on a board and smeared with a *thin* layer of vaseline (if it's too thick you run the risk of making the head soft).

Pieces of gauze the size of large postage-stamps are moistened with synthetic resin glue, laid on to the two halves of the head and smoothed on with a brush. Each layer must get quite dry before the next is put on. There should be at least four covering layers and more if the head is very big.

47

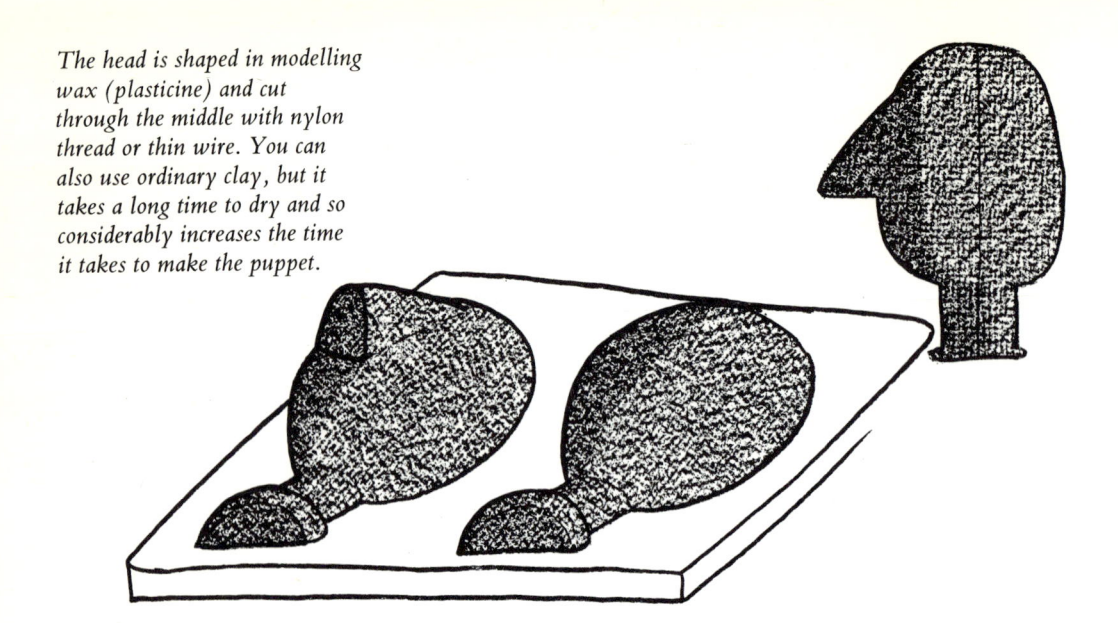

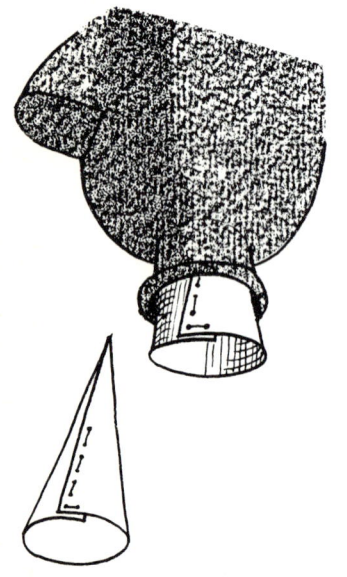

The head is shaped in modelling wax (plasticine) and cut through the middle with nylon thread or thin wire. You can also use ordinary clay, but it takes a long time to dry and so considerably increases the time it takes to make the puppet.

A cloth finger-stall must be placed in the hollow head, or you will have no way to hold it.

When the gauze is quite dry and hard you scrape the modelling wax out. (Don't worry if the gauze gets a bit soft; this helps when the two halves are put together. If necessary you can strengthen the gauze with an extra smoothing layer, which is allowed to dry without the modelling wax.)

The two halves are glued together with several layers of gauze. It's rather a delicate operation to make the joint look nice as the head has a habit of collapsing. Put the head on a stick and stand the stick in a bottle, so that the head can stand and dry. Watch out that it doesn't collapse while it's drying – take a look at it now and then.

When quite dry the head can be smoothed over with gauze and glue. If you like the rough gauze surface the head can now be painted with plastic paints. If you prefer a smoother surface, it can be coated with two more layers of tissue paper and glue before painting.

A finger-stall is sewn out of strong material (for example canvas) so that it fits over the finger or fingers that are to work the puppet's head. Sew it cone-shaped, using carpet-thread. The finger-stall is stuck up into the neck and fastened in the same way with carpet-thread to the puppet's neck. Since the needle has to go through the puppet's gauze covering, it must be a strong one (perhaps a saddle-maker's needle).

Two puppets from Kjeld Iversen's puppet play 'Fly then Man'. Majken Jacoby made them out of glued gauze over modelling wax. The tree is cut out from cloth mounted on velvet and net.

The rod is fastened in a hollow puppet's head with large-headed nails. It's best to give the head a long neck about as thick as the rod. If necessary it can be adjusted with glue and gauze.

Rod puppet with arms of spring curtain-rod. If the dress is made of a piece of net the puppet will shake and look very lifelike when moved with small jerks of the rod.

ROD PUPPETS

The method described above is best suited to glove puppets, since the head is hollow. If you make a long neck (without a collar) which fits the thickness of the rod, don't use too thin a stick. You can, however, use glue and small nails to fix the rod to the hollow head – but only with big heads. If the rod doesn't fit snugly in the neck it can be made thicker with glue and bits of gauze. You also cover the joint between the neck and the rod with glue and gauze.

BODIES

ROD PUPPETS AND THEIR CLOTHES

Once you've made a head on a stick, you have got the basic form of a rod puppet, which can be used in many ways.

A piece of curtain-spring can be fixed across the rod so that the puppet has arms that go up and down when you move it. You can sew hands and fit them to the arms. You can hang some material or furs over the arms, and then the puppet is dressed.

You can also make a coat for the rod puppet from two pieces of strong material (for example linen) in the shape of big Ts (see drawing) and hem the material along the dotted lines on the picture. The Ts are sewn together all the way round except at the thick lines marked *a*.

The rod with its head is put through the neck-hole of the coat. When it is at the right height the coat is fastened to the rod with a drawing-pin at the back of the neck. The rod and the coat must be fastened together at this one point only, otherwise the head can't turn freely.

Over the rod puppet's coat you can put more elegant clothes and ornaments; the coat is a basis on which to hang the more frivolous items of clothing.

A thread can also be sewn firmly on to the neck of the coat, at the back. Then, using a long needle (see the list of materials at the back of the book), the thread is sewn through the puppet's head. A big knot at the top of the head prevents the thread from slipping out again.

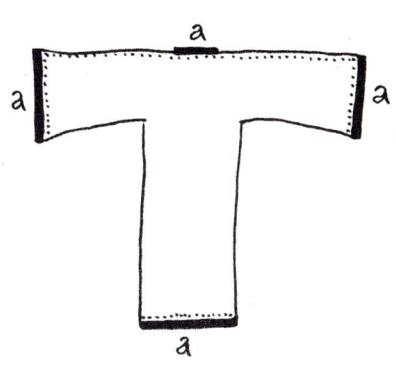

A shirt or frock is made from two identical pieces of material using this pattern.

THE PUPPET'S HANDS

Hands in the shape of small mittens can be made from material. They are stuffed with something like foam rubber and sewn to the arms of the coat. You can also cut out hands from wood or polystyrene/styrafoam, covering the foam with glue and gauze as you did with the head.

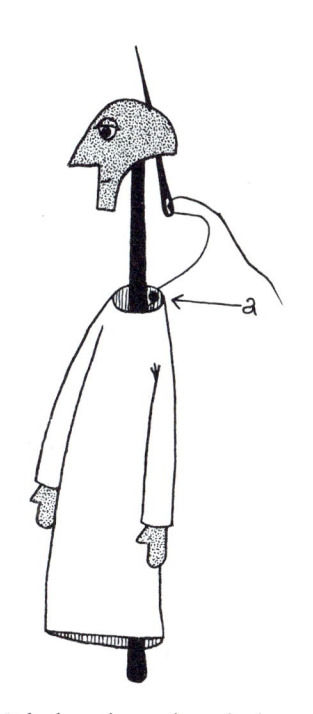

ACTION RODS

The arms and hands can be controlled with two rods. These might be made of aluminium (see the description of materials, under metal rods), but you can also use other metals or wooden sticks. Aluminium is suggested because it is easy to work and doesn't weigh much. On the other hand it gets bent easily, which can be rather a nuisance when the puppets are being moved from place to place. However, the rods are easily straightened out again.

It looks rather awkward when the needle is sticking through the puppet's head, and it needs a long needle. But it can be done. It helps if the needle is warmed when the head is made of polystyrene.

The action rods must be of the same length as the rod that forms the puppet's backbone, preferably about 2 ft. 3 in. (70 cm.), and about $\frac{1}{8}$ in. (4 mm.) in diameter.

Using a hammer, beat the aluminium rods flat at one end. You can use the head of another hammer as an anvil. In the end you have flattened, bore a hole with a metal drill. It should be about $\frac{1}{16}$ in. (2 mm.) in diameter.

If the hands are of cloth, the action rods are sewn to them as shown in the picture on the right. If the hands are of wood or polystyrene/styrafoam they are fixed to the rods with an eyelet and string, or with a nail. The rods mustn't be fixed too firmly to the hands or their movement will be restricted.

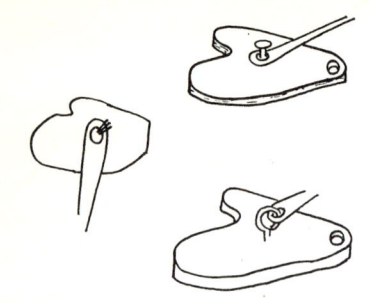

On the left, a cloth hand with the rod sewn to it. On the right, two wooden or glued gauze hands. Here the rod can either be attached with a nail (above) or with an eyelet.

Rod puppets from the puppet play 'The Golden Toad'. The heads and hands are made of polystyrene covered with glued gauze, as described on page 44. The arms are worked with aluminium rods.

A puppet manipulator can easily manage a rod puppet of this kind. He either works the puppet's two arms with one hand, or he lets one of the puppet's hands hang down loosely while he concentrates on the other. If two manipulators are available, one of them holds the head and body while the other works the arms.

POLYSTYRENE/STYRAFOAM BODY

The rod puppet's body can, as mentioned on page 50, be a coat which can be made in a number of ways. But you can also carve the body out of polystyrene and coat it with gauze and glue like the heads. Then the puppet's backbone has to be stuck through the body and into the head. On the body you can put loose, dangling arms made of string or other flexible material. The hands and the action rods are fitted as described above. Both body, hands and head can be painted with plastic paints.

If you make rod puppets entirely of gauze and glue as just described they may well work rather stiffly. On the other hand, it's possible to make puppets which are effective precisely because of their mechanical appearance.

The body can also be made of polystyrene covered with glued gauze.

53

The puppet can only nod, but he's pretty good at that!

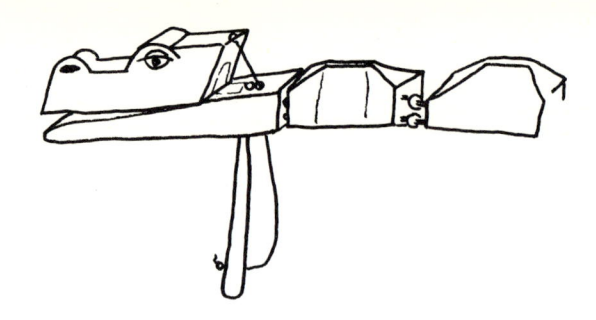

The boa constrictor can open its jaw threateningly. Its body consists of a long row of joints made of polystyrene covered with glued gauze. The joints are sewn together.

The two puppets in the drawing come, like the puppet with curtain-spring arms on page 50, from a puppet play called 'Prip and Prop' (see also page 38), for which all the puppets were purposely made mechanical but very simple.

The moving parts of a puppet of this kind can be joined together by means of a wide piece of sticking plaster or linen tape. The sticking plaster will work as a hinge and three or four layers of glued gauze are stuck over the plaster to make the hinge firm. By simply pulling a string one of the puppets in the picture can be made to nod and the other to open its mouth. The string is fastened and drawn through metal eyelets and finally pulled through a hole in the action rod and knotted so that it can't slip out.

GLOVE PUPPETS

When you make a glove puppet's body you must be careful that the operator's hand doesn't get lost in all the seams, folds, joints and so on. You must give it an undergarment, in the form of a glove of strong material (cotton or linen) sewn in a single piece. Outside this underclothing you can go to town with every kind of decoration, ornament and frippery by way of clothes. Without the undergarment the dresses will soon fall to pieces with use.

THE SHAPE OF THE GLOVE

We start by drawing a pattern from which the cloth can be cut. The outline of this pattern depends first and foremost on the puppet manipulator's hand and on which fingers he wants to use to control the puppet's head and arms.

Lay your hand and arm on a piece of paper with the fingers as they are when you are working the puppet. Draw the outline up to the elbow, leaving plenty of room on all sides. Find the centre line down through the outline and fold along this line (*a* to *a* in the drawing). Now cut the folded pattern out, following the line that encloses the larger area. The cut-out pattern, which is symmetrical, constitutes one half of a glove. The paper is now used as a paper pattern to cut out two identical pieces of cloth which are sewn together to form a glove.

You must remember a number of things when you're drawing the pattern. The puppet must have short, wide arms which your fingers can reach into easily. The puppet's arms have to catch hold of objects and do a whole lot more.

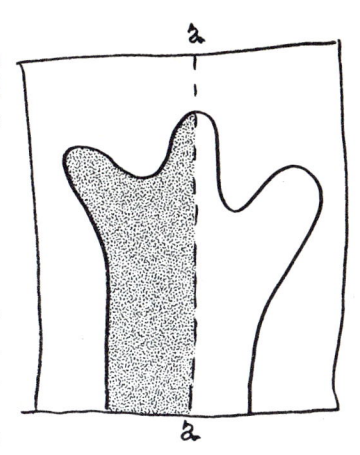

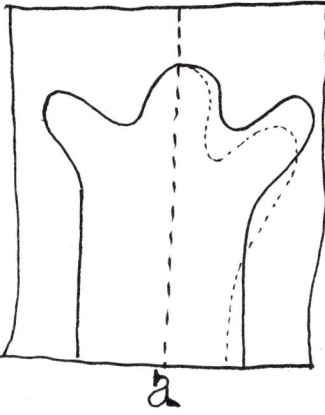

Top, the 'crooked' outline drawn round the hand. The paper is folded down the middle, a–a. Bottom, the 'glove', which is cut out double following the half that leaves most room for the hand. This way you make a symmetrical glove. You do not cut along the dotted line on the right of the drawing.

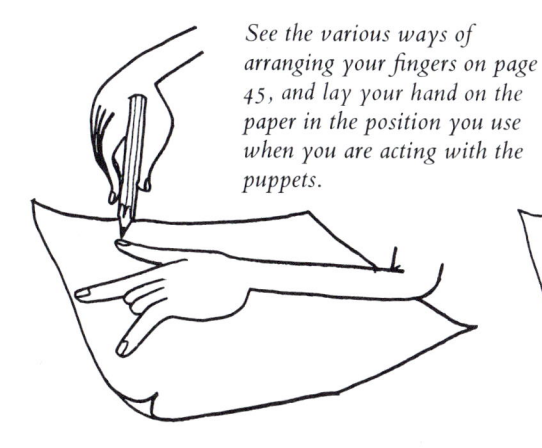

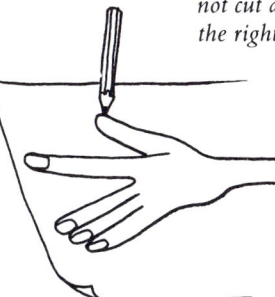

See the various ways of arranging your fingers on page 45, and lay your hand on the paper in the position you use when you are acting with the puppets.

55

A glove puppet can quite easily have legs. They are sewn as stuffed rolls of cloth and fastened to the bottom of the glove. Tony has a bit of old fur for hair. He is talking to a washing-up brush, which has wooden eyes, nose and mouth, and can slide its head up and down in its rod puppet dress (see page 50). (The puppets are from 'Tony in the Whistling Marsh' by Helle Ryslinge and Tom Nagel Rasmussen.)

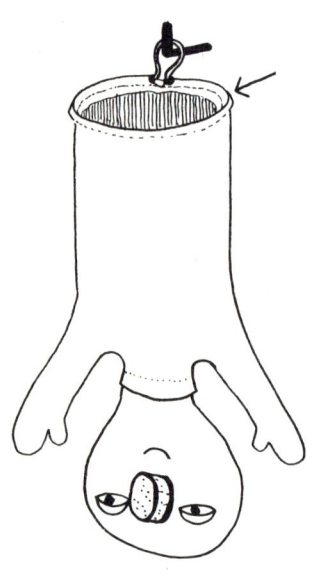

The puppet is easy to put on if there is a wire ring sewn round the bottom of the glove.

It's better to make the glove too wide than too narrow; you can always make a couple of folds in the back or front afterwards if you find you're lost in it, and a good big glove also hides the occasional tilts that the hand must give to the puppet's body.

And make sure there's plenty of room in the neck. When it's finished you need to make a hem and thread elastic through it so that the body can be fixed to the head.

Two pieces of cloth are now cut out following the pattern (allow for the hem) and sewn together all the way round except at the bottom where the hand has to go, and the top where the puppet's head will fit on.

You can sew in round the bottom some fine wire shaped into a ring, so that you can get the puppet on to your hand quickly. When the clothes are sewn on outside the glove, be careful you don't put your hand into the wrong part by mistake.

PUTTING ON THE HEAD

If the puppet's head is fitted with a little rod, the glove is put on as described under rod puppets (page 51). If the head has a finger-hole and a neck with the collar, the hem just mentioned is sewn and threaded with elastic. The elastic is stretched over the neck of the puppet's head (*b* in the picture). The glove will stay on firmly because of the collar but can still be taken off to put new clothes on the puppet. However, if you prefer you can sew the glove firmly to the puppet's head all round the neck.

OTHER PUPPETS

There is no limit to the number of different types of puppets and hybrids of these types. Some people don't like mixing the different kinds of puppets: glove puppets, rod puppets, marionettes, shadow puppets and the rest. Others feel that it is these very mixtures that create so many possibilities for building up plays. In the long run, it is a question of one's own style or artistic preference rather than a question of historical or technical categories.

So if we don't in this book discuss all kinds of puppet, and leave out, for example, marionettes, this is not on principle but simply because it is too wide a subject to include everything. Marionettes would need a whole book to themselves.

We will, however, briefly discuss some puppets which are closely related to glove and rod puppets. They are worked from below like the other puppets in this book (whereas marionettes are worked from above) and they go well in company with the puppets we've already described.

If there is a collar on the puppet's head, elastic threaded through the hem round the neck of the glove makes the glove stay on. And it is easy to change the puppet's clothes.

THE MAROTTE

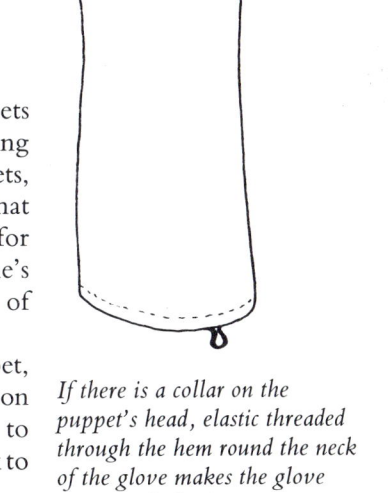

The marotte is really just a simple form of rod puppet. The head is fitted on to a rod and it is made over a balloon. The balloon mustn't be blown up too much. Bits of gauze dipped in synthetic resin glue are glued on to it and up to five or six layers may be necessary. The air leaks out of the balloon by itself while the gauze dries, and the head can easily be taken off. A rod is fastened in the hollow head in a cardboard roll, as shown on page 50. A coat-hanger without a hook is fitted on to the rod, so that the puppet can be dressed in a shirt or blouse. If you like you can stuff the shirt with a cushion.

The hands are the actor's own, sticking out from the puppet's body.

If there is only the one actor, he holds the head and body in one hand and makes the other hand become the puppet's. The puppet is one-armed. The other arm just hangs down, and if you like it can be stuffed. If there are two actors, one can hold the head and body and the other can stick both his hands forward as the puppet's. This makes the puppet much more lifelike, especially when it is doing something like scratching its head or holding a stick. The puppeteer can hide behind the puppet or take part in the act; he may for instance talk to the puppet like a ventriloquist. The marotte is usually nearly life-size.

CLOTH PUPPETS

Cloth puppets are really a development of bag puppets and they make good puppet animals. Their most essential feature is their huge jaws, which are sewn over a kind of

The frogs are stuffed. They can only open and shut their mouths, but they do that very entertainingly, since the soft material together with the hand stuck in the head makes a splendid imitation possible. (From 'Tony in the Whistling Marsh', by Helle Ryslinge and Tom Nagel Rasmussen.)

Ester Nagel's 'Hatfather' from her comedy 'Hovsa and Tralle' can both scratch his head and play the piano. But he needs the actor's help. The puppet's nose and eyes are 'bumps' from egg-trays covered over with glued gauze. Hair and beard are made out of wool, which on this puppet is first glued on to tapes. Hair can also be made out of such things as raffia, cotton wool or shavings, glued on with synthetic resin glue.

The elephant is made from corduroy. Its eyes are buttons, the tusks are candles. One actor holds the head and makes it open its mouth. Another actor has the two legs on his arms. A puppet like this can be worked by one actor if he puts the puppet's head on his own head and the legs on his arms, but then of course the animal won't be able to open its mouth! (The puppet was made by Majken Jacoby for Kjeld Iversen's puppet-play 'Fly then Man'.)

mitten. The thumb goes in the lower jaw and the other fingers in the upper.

If the puppet is sewn over a glove with fingers, the different fingers can give the animal some very expressive mouth movements.

The thumb is kept in the lower jaw, but the other fingers may, for example, work a tongue that can stick out and lick, or make the upper lip quiver, pout or grimace.

The bull can do very well without hair—but it looks pretty funny with raffia hair.

HAIR AND BEARD

It's incredible what hair and a beard can do for a puppet's appearance (and a man's too, come to that). The simplest thing is to paint hair and beard on the puppet, but once you've begun sticking raffia, wool, fur, cotton yarn and so

String hair, just like real hair, has to be held out of your eyes if you want to see.

61

MONOLOGUE

'My dear spectators. May I have the pleasure of bidding you welcome with this speech – also called a monologue. You see me here like a pearl in this little puppet theatre, which I call mine because no one else makes any claim on it. I am not only the star of the theatre. I am also its manager. I will do everything to ensure that you enjoy yourselves. This temple of the theatrical art will not be entered by crude and uncultivated want of talent. Unfortunately I am at present alone in the theatre. Many have sought entrance, but they lacked education and artistic qualities.

Just think, ladies and gentlemen. They actually tried to palm off a pair of old shoes on me! There ought to be puppets, or marionettes as I prefer to call them. Luckily I am in the fortunate situation that I can today introduce you to a properly qualified candidate, made in a proper puppet workshop. I expect him any minute.'

Now the new puppet comes forward. He pops up from the audience's side and goes towards the theatre with his operator.

DIALOGUE

'I'm sorry. You must have come to the wrong place.'

'They said there was an old duck who was in charge of a flea circus. She was looking for marionettes for her theatre.'

'An old duck? You can't mean me?'

'Sorry about that, old dear. You look fairly harmless anyway – you don't bite. But then you haven't got a tooth in your mouth.'

'Will you be so kind as to take a voice test up here in the theatre?'

'Is that old wardrobe a theatre? It stinks of mothballs.'

'So you wish to have an audition, or do you not?'

'Okay, okay! So long as you don't draw the curtain, so I get hurt.'

The actor goes up to the theatre with the new puppet. He goes in and the puppet appears on the playboard beside the prima donna.

The prima donna.

A FAIRY TALE

'What shall we act, auntie?'
'A nice fairy tale, I should think. With poetic and powerful speeches to delight the beholders.'
'Good, let's go. Once upon a time there was a soldier. He was in love with a beautiful young princess. We must have a princess.'
'A princess? That's me!'
'No, no, you're the manager. You sit in the booking-office. You manage. I'll begin again. Once upon a time there was a rich princess. She was old and ugly, but the soldier had a passion for her because she had so much money.'

'Well, I never! I don't care for that at all. You are a vulgar person. Get out. You're fired.'

'Good, good. There isn't room to move in this little box anyway. I want a whole room for my theatre. Come up and see me some time. Then you'll really see a theatre.'

He leaves the theatre and goes out of the room. The prima donna is alone again.

EPILOGUE

'Ladies and gentlemen of the audience, you must please forgive this painful episode. I must have applied to the wrong agents. I will do better in the future. I hope it was not too unpleasant for you. You can get your money back at the entrance. We will try to prepare something new next time you come.'

She bows, and the curtain falls to the sound of a fanfare.

More Theatres

Now what? The prima donna is disappointed with her little puppet theatre. She wonders what the matter is. Since there can't be anything wrong with her, it must be the theatre. It isn't grand enough. It's too small. You can see into it from the sides. There's no scenery or proper lighting, and the curtain can't be raised and lowered properly. What shall she do now?

THE PRIMA DONNA'S THEATRE AND THE NEW PUPPET'S THEATRE

The prima donna is her operator's first puppet. He made her and now he caresses her. He builds a new theatre for her. You can see how he builds it on the next pages.

The beginning of a puppet theatre built from a construction set.

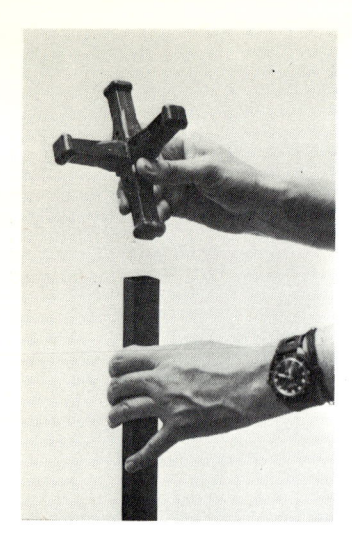

Rod and junction.

But the new puppet, who had to give up his easy job with the prima donna, is also building a theatre. He gets *his* operator to help him. Apart from anything else, it will infuriate the prima donna.

CONSTRUCTION FRAMES

The construction frame is a system of metal rods and parts, normally used for shop furnishing (for example 'Speed Frame', see page 88).

It is possible to build puppet theatres in various sizes using this type of system. Here we examine the building of a fairly small theatre which doesn't take up much room and which can be packed away so that it takes up little or no space.

MATERIALS

The materials recommended here will enable you to build both an open and a closed theatre. The difference in materials and preparations is not great, and it makes it possible for a variety show with puppets to move between two kinds of stage.

For the open theatre you need to buy the following parts:
10 rods 5 ft. $2\frac{1}{4}$ in. (58.1 cm.)
9 rods 2 ft. $7\frac{1}{2}$ in. (79.2 cm.)
10 junctions.

In addition, material for the proscenium:
1 piece 4 ft. 3 in. × 3 ft. 3 in. (130 × 100 cm.)

Material for the back curtain:
1 piece 3 ft. 3 in. × 3 ft. 3 in. (100 × 100 cm.).

The material must be hard-wearing and preferably not shiny. Shiny materials reflect the light and may distract attention from what is happening on the stage. For the same reason you will usually want to use material of a single colour; for example a lightweight flannel is very suitable. Otherwise you can equip the theatre how you like. If you want ornamental curtains, you can use patterned material or decorate the plain material in various ways – with strips of cloth (sewn on or glued with, for instance, Bostik or

Uhu), by painting the material (paints for this purpose can be bought at the paint suppliers or craft materials shop and the material should preferably be of a light colour), with embroidery (using thick wool) and so on.

Further requirements are:
1 board about $\frac{3}{8}$ in. (1 cm.) thick, measuring 3 ft. 3 in. × 6 in. (100 × 15 cm.) for the playboard or stage.
1 board about $\frac{3}{8}$ in. (1 cm.) thick, measuring 3 ft. 3 in. × $3\frac{1}{4}$ in. (100 × 8 cm.) for the back curtain.

A RUBBER OR WOODEN HAMMER

At first the rods and junctions may be a bit tight, but they can be knocked together with a rubber or wooden hammer (a bit of wood can also be used). It is important not to use an ordinary hammer which makes dents in the rods. Later, when they have been assembled and dismantled a number of times they will become looser. If they get too loose they can be tightened by knocking the rods a little flat at the junctions.

AN OPEN THEATRE

A junction is fitted at one end of each of the eight short rods. (See the photograph.)

Make a 'table' out of four of these rods, using them as legs, and use four long rods to form the sides of the table. See the drawing, where the free points of the junctions are marked with the letter *a*.

Now make another, similar table and fit it over the first, as shown in the drawing. With two short and two long rods plus two junctions a 'bridge' is built and put above the upper 'table', so that the whole thing begins to look like a chair without a seat. The 'bridge' will then be the back of the chair (see the drawing).

We shall now use the two boards measuring 3 ft. 3 in. × $3\frac{1}{4}$ in. × $\frac{3}{8}$ in. (100 × 8 × 1 cm.) and 3 ft. 3 in. × 6 in. × $\frac{3}{8}$ in. (100 × 15 × 1 cm.). Bore holes in them $\frac{1}{2}$ in. (1.3 cm.) across, $3\frac{7}{8}$ in. (9.75 cm.) from the short side and $1\frac{5}{8}$ in. (4 cm.) from one of the long sides. These holes will be the right size for the free points of the junctions to go through them.

The parts can be knocked together with a piece of wood if you haven't got a rubber or wooden hammer.

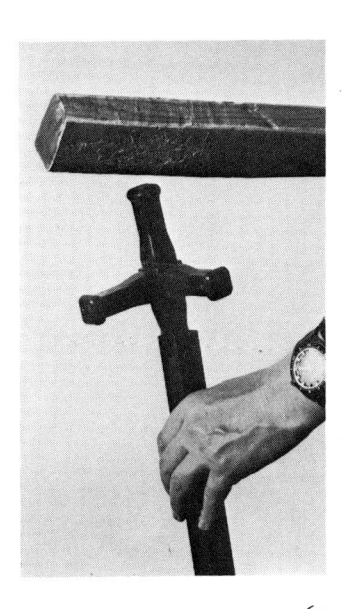

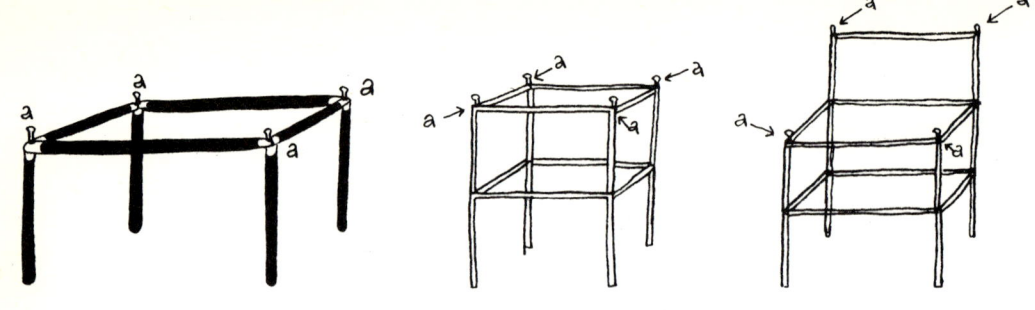

Left, the first 'table'. Centre, a table has been built on top. Right, the table is fitted with a back, so that it looks like a chair.

The top parts of the table are put on and the metal framework is complete.

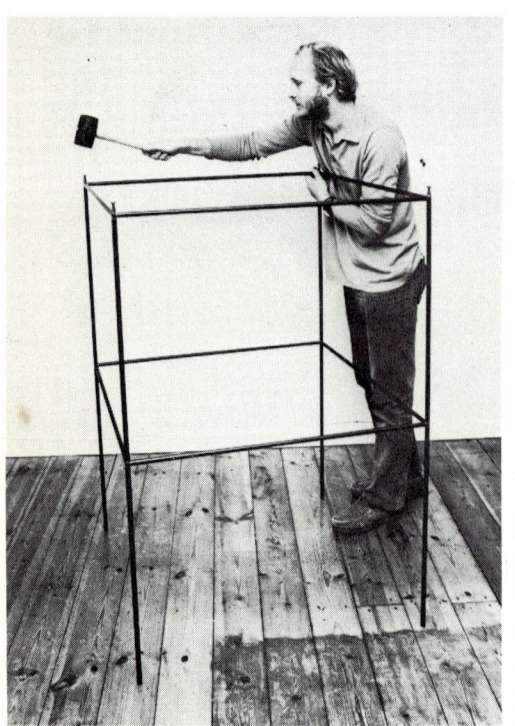

On the narrow board the back curtain is securely nailed. On the other you nail the big proscenium curtain measuring 4 ft. 3 in. × 3 ft. 3 in. (130 × 100 cm.) so that the curtain is attached to the long side near the two holes. (Use small nails with big heads, such as tacks.)

The two boards with the curtains look the same except that the proscenium curtain is twice as long as the back curtain and is nailed to the broader of the two boards (the playboard). See the drawing, where *a* is the board and *b* is the curtain. The board with the back curtain is fitted to the back of the 'chair' and the board with the proscenium curtain is fitted to the front side of the seat of the 'chair'. The theatre now looks as shown in the drawing.

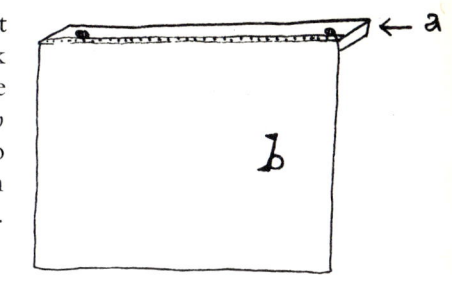

The back curtain nailed to the narrow board.

THE PUPPETS IN THE OPEN THEATRE

The actor sits in this theatre just as he did in the blind-frame theatre (see page 36). A chair or a box is used of the right height for the actor, so that his head is just not seen from

The completed theatre as the audience see it. The two boards are marked a and the two curtains b.

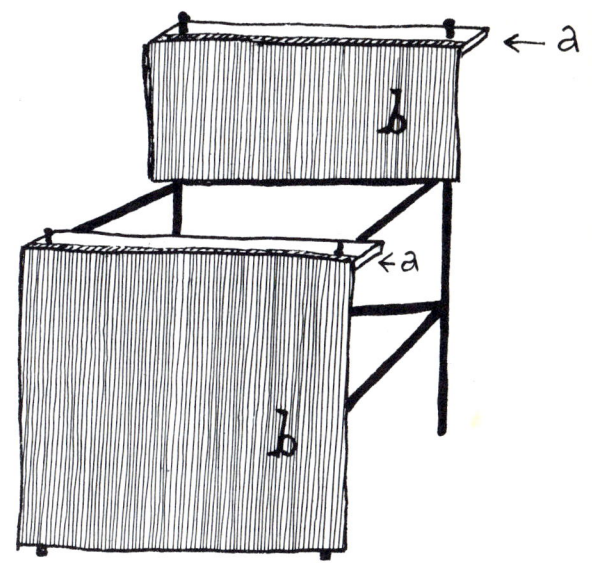

The completed theatre photographed without the front curtain, so that the whole construction can be seen.

71

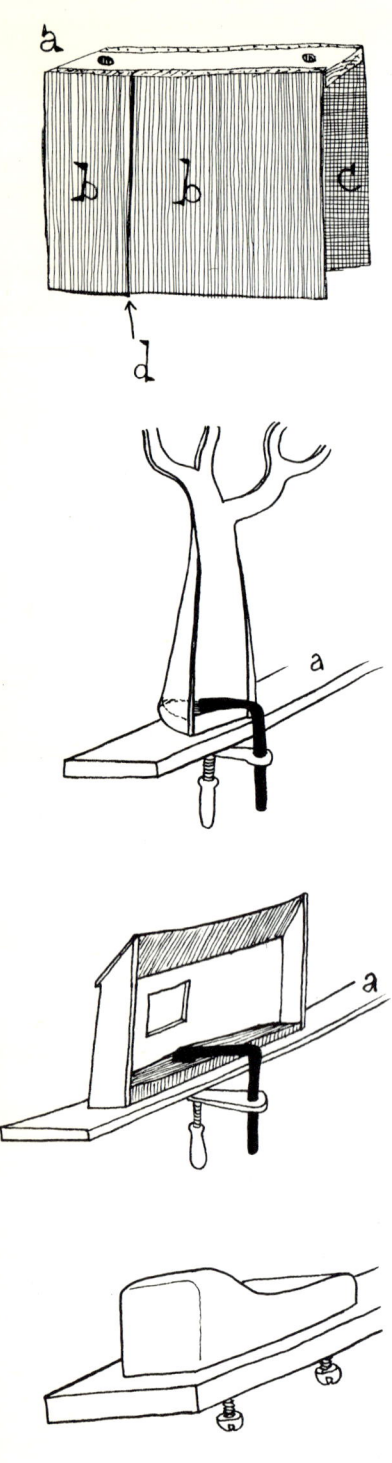

outside. In the photograph the actor is sitting a little too high! If you like you can use a chair on wheels, or screw wheels that will turn (for example piano castors) under the box as mentioned in connection with the blind-frame theatre. This gives great mobility. Small children can, if preferred, stand up in the theatre.

The puppets can move around freely on the ramp. However, they have to come up out of the depths. You can make the back curtain of two pieces of material, which needn't be of the same width and make the puppets come on through the curtains. To prevent people seeing right through the theatre when the puppets come forward from behind the curtain, you can make an extra back curtain. This is nailed on the back side of the back curtain board, as sketched in the drawing, where *b* is the double curtain and *c* is the extra back curtain; *a* is the board.

SCENERY AND LIGHTING

The back curtain can be decorated as scenery (see page 58). You can make several back curtains of this kind, each mounted on its own board, so that you can change them around.

They can be moved quite openly by one of the actors during the play. You simply lift the board from the junction, back curtain and all, and put a new one on.

Smaller pieces of scenery can be fitted on the playboard. They can be cut out of strong cardboard with a Stanley knife or similar tool or sawn out of plywood or hardboard with a fretsaw.

How these properties are attached depends on their shape. From an ironmonger you can get small screwclips or vices which are useful for this and many other purposes.

The drawings show, top, a tree cut out of strong cardcardboard; it is bent round a semicircular piece of wood, glued to it with synthetic resin glue and further secured with nails, so that the tree has a round trunk. The wooden plate is fixed firmly to the ramp *a* with a screw clip. The middle drawing shows a house secured in the same way. The bottom drawing shows a divan which is cut out of polystyrene/styrafoam and screwed on to a piece of wood which, again, can be fastened to the stage with a screw clip.

The lighting comes from reading lamps or photographic lamps, which are fitted in front of the theatre or at the sides in the way described for the earlier kinds of puppet theatre.

THE CLOSED THEATRE

If you want to build a closed theatre you can build on to the theatre just described, using the following additional materials:
2 junctions
2 rods 1 ft. $10\frac{3}{4}$ in. (58.1 cm.)
2 rods 2 ft. $7\frac{1}{4}$ in. (79.2 cm.)
1 board of $\frac{3}{8}$ in. × 3 ft. 3 in. × 6 in. (1 × 100 × 15 cm.)
together with three pieces of material each measuring 3 ft. 3 in. × 8 in. (100 × 20 cm.).

A 'bridge' is fitted above the playboard. It is made of the two short rods, placed vertically, and one long, placed above horizontally. The legs of the bridge go through the

The little puppet theatre has been turned into a big theatre! The big theatre before the sides are enclosed.

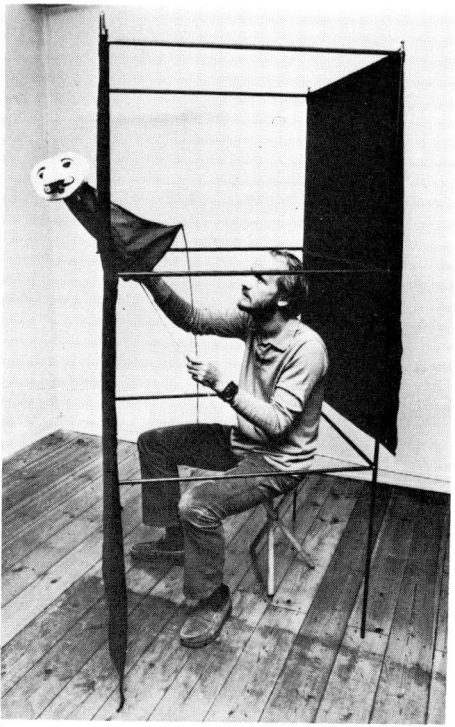

This is what the frame looks like.

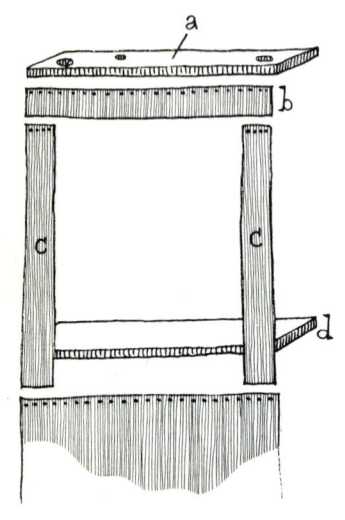

The separate parts of the proscenium.

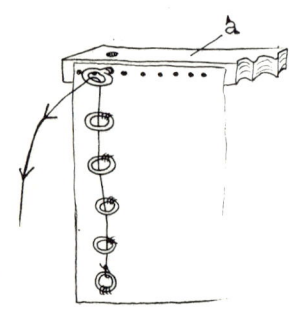

How the rings are attached.

two holes in the playboard and down to the junction. The two bridges are then joined with the two remaining long rods. In the drawing the new rods are shown in outline, while the frame of the old theatre is in black.

The original back curtain, which you have taken off while building up the frame, is now put back again. All that remains is to make a new stage opening. The three pieces of material of the same size, i.e. 3 ft. 3 in. × 8 in. (100 × 20 cm.) and the board of $\frac{3}{8}$ in. × 3 ft. 3 in. × 6 in. (1 × 100 × 15 cm.) will form the top part of the proscenium.

The board is given $\frac{1}{2}$ in. (1.3 cm.) holes as the other board (the playboard) was, with perhaps an extra hole for an electric lead; they will be $3\frac{7}{8}$ in. (9.75 cm.) from the short surface and $1\frac{5}{8}$ in. (4 cm.) from the front side. Then two of the strips of material *c* are sewn on so that they hang down from the board (see the drawing); the last piece of material is sewn across above them *b*. Now the top part of the proscenium can be hung in position.

If you want to close the theatre from the audience even more you may fit it with two side curtains. These must both be 5 ft. 11 in. × 2 ft. 6 in. (180 × 75 cm.).

Both curtains need to have a hem on the short side, so that they can be drawn on to the two long rods which connect the bridges (see above, assembly of the frame of the closed theatre). You must pull these side curtains on to the rods *while* the 'bridges' are being connected. Now you are completely hidden from the audience, the only place where you are not surrounded by curtains is at the back below the back curtain, which can be a sort of stage entrance.

THE FRONT CURTAIN

On the back of the board *a*, which carries the highest part of the proscenium, you can nail a stage curtain. It can be a piece of material on the back of which you have sewn five or six vertical rows of curtain rings. Strings of thin, plaited nylon cord, are tied to the bottom rings and pulled up through the other rings, as shown in the sketch. All the strings lead to one of the sides and are gathered in a knot round a hook, so that you only have to pull one string when the curtain goes up. The hook for the end of the strings can be fixed to one of the side rods of the theatre when the curtain is pulled up. Then it will stay in position during the performance.

You can also divide the stage curtain into two. In this case the rings must be sewn on diagonally. They will start at the bottom inside corner and extend to the top outside corner; a string is tied to the lowest ring and threaded through the others. Two eyelets are fastened to the board, one on each side (see the drawing). The strings are pulled through them and gathered together on one side, where they hang down. A hook can hold the curtain up in the same way as before.

You can of course simply sew a curtain rod on to the board and sew rings on the top edge of the curtain, which can then be drawn by hand. A ready-made system of curtain rings meant for curtains can be bought from a hardware shop.

If you sew a metal chain (a piece of lavatory chain, for instance) along the bottom of the curtain, the weight of it will hold the curtain in position when it falls at the end of the performance.

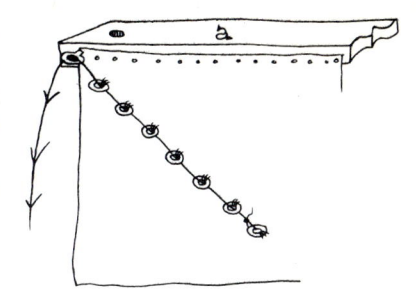

Arrangement of rings for the divided front curtain.

LIGHTING

If you wish to install electrical equipment you may set up your own circuit, but make sure that before connecting it to the mains you have it checked by your local electricity board. Assemble everything before checking – this will make it less expensive.

For lighting, you need:
2 boards of $\frac{3}{8}$ in. × 3 ft. × 4 in. (1 × 90 × 10 cm.)
3 small sockets
3 small bulbs
flex and plug.

The top board, which carries the front curtain and the upper part of the proscenium, can also be used to hang the lighting on.

A small electric socket is attached to the underside An eyelet is screwed into the board and the socket is fixed into the eye-hole with an electrician's screw and nut. A lead is fixed and taken up through the hole in the board so that it runs along the upper side of the board. Between the board and the bulb you stick a piece of tinfoil (which can be glued with Bostik) so that the bulb doesn't scorch the wood. Be careful too that the curtain doesn't get scorched when it's pulled up.

Photographic or other kinds of lamps can easily be fitted to the frame of the theatre. Lamps similar to the one in the photograph can be bought at any good electrical shop.

Several boards with lamps can be fitted across the upper frame of the theatre. They are laid over it quite loosely. Valances (narrow cloth runners) should be nailed to the front side of these boards, otherwise the light from the bulbs gets in the eyes of the audience. The valances also prevent the audience from seeing right up to the ceiling if they're sitting in the front row.

With this kind of lighting system you can practically do without spotlights (reading lamps or photographic lamps) from the front. Only if the puppets come right up to the front of the playboard is there a danger that their faces may be a little in the dark.

SCENERY

You can make many different kinds of scenery by laying round sticks with flats sewn on to them cross-wise over the top of the theatre. The first drawing shows this system in its simplest form; the next shows a room where the puppets can come in through a door in the scenery itself.

The scenes can also be cut out of coloured material and sewn, glued or ironed on to black net. If they are ironed, you use a piece of Vilene as a layer between the decorations

A scene made from cloth cut-outs on black net is hung up. The character stands behind the net but can be seen through the light material.

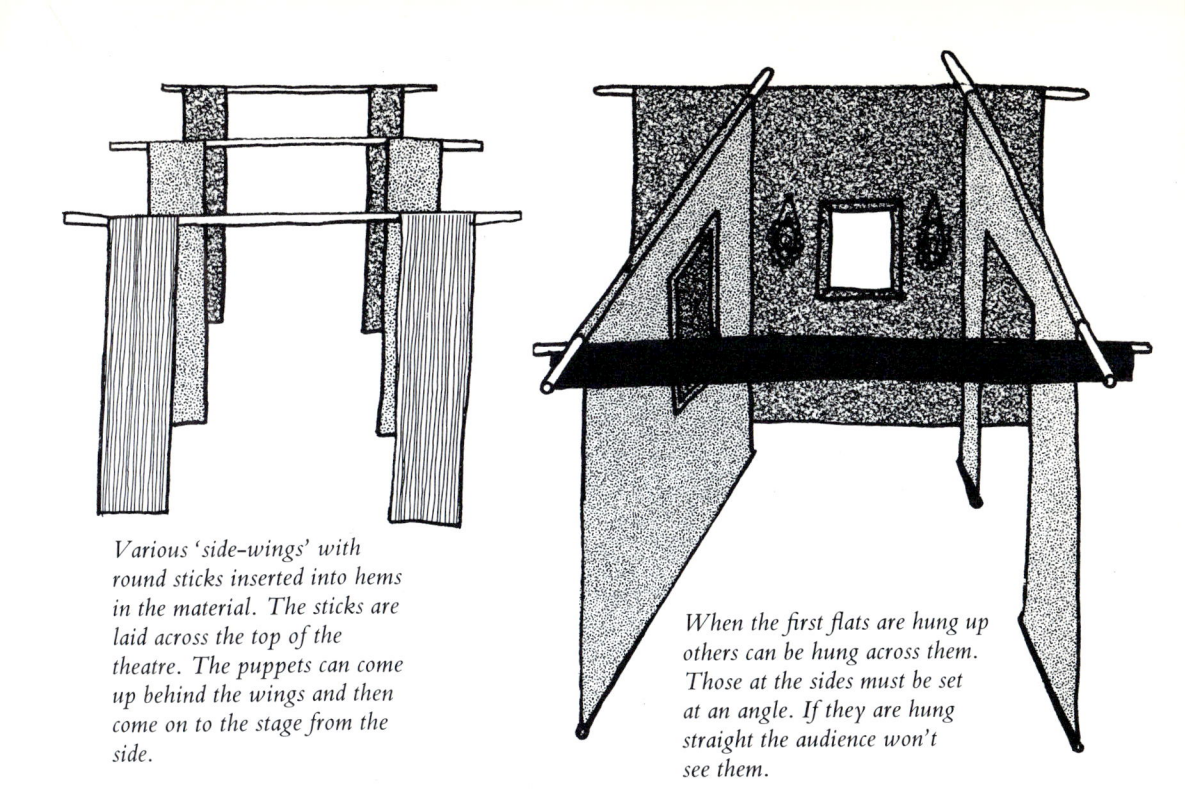

Various 'side-wings' with round sticks inserted into hems in the material. The sticks are laid across the top of the theatre. The puppets can come up behind the wings and then come on to the stage from the side.

When the first flats are hung up others can be hung across them. Those at the sides must be set at an angle. If they are hung straight the audience won't see them.

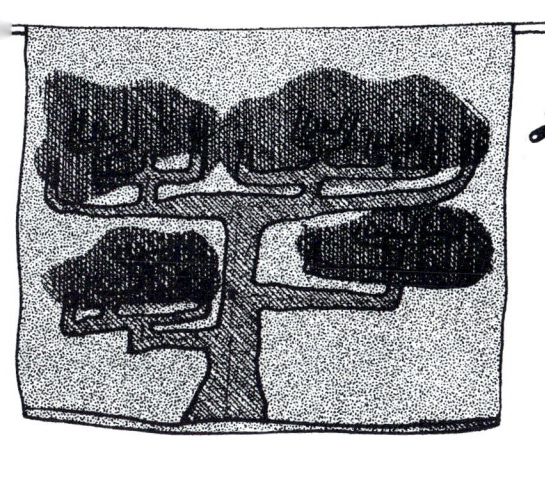

Cut-outs on black net. By inserting a round stick into a hem the scene is hung over the top of the theatre.

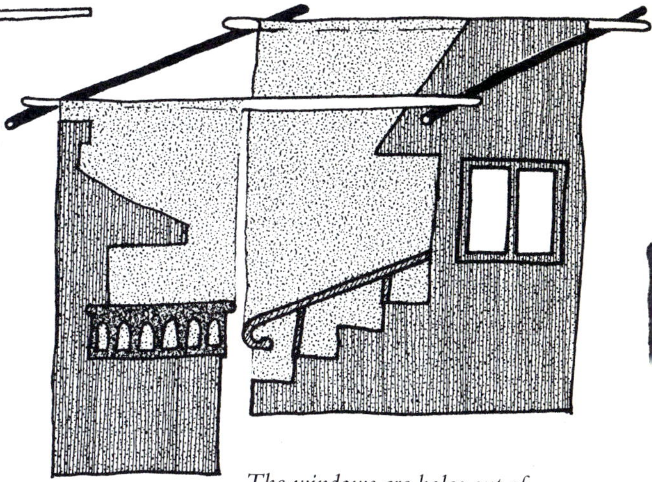

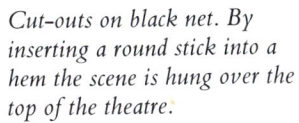

The houses are cut out of different materials (or, if preferred, painted on canvas with oil paints) and sewn on to black net. The puppets can still be seen behind the net.

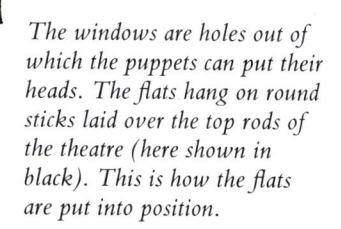

The windows are holes out of which the puppets can put their heads. The flats hang on round sticks laid over the top rods of the theatre (here shown in black). This is how the flats are put into position.

and the net. Black net will be transparent and invisible to the audience.

In the drawings you can see a tree and a house which have been ironed on to net. In the windows of the house the net has been cut away so that the puppets can put their heads out.

The back curtain can be changed as for the open theatre, but you can also hang opaque flats up in front of it. They are sewn on round sticks like the other flats and form new back cloths.

THE PUPPETS IN THE CLOSED THEATRE

The actor gets into position as for the open theatre. For instructions on the control of the puppets, see page 36 (the blind-frame theatre). The puppets have less room to move than in the open theatre and the audience must sit straight in front of the stage, which isn't necessary with the open theatre. On the other hand, the traditional closed theatre makes it possible to hang up flats in various ways and to create an attractive scene in conjunction with lighting effects; in the closed theatre the puppets can tumble about in front of, behind and among the scenery with new lighting on them the whole time.

BIGGER THEATRES

The building system employed here can be used to build bigger theatres. You can get stronger, four-sided rods with junctions to correspond. You can also buy projectors to go with the system which can be fitted directly on to the rods.

OTHER THEATRES

Besides the one described here there are other metal rod systems which can be used for building puppet theatres. There are systems which, unlike the one mentioned, are specifically designed for puppet theatres. They are a bit more expensive, but extremely good. You can also build your own system from wooden rods, square-sectioned rods with holes for nuts and bolts for example, so that the theatre can be easily erected and dismantled.

You can also, of course, build a theatre from wooden sheets, but it will be heavy. However, this shouldn't matter much if the theatre doesn't have to be moved.

THEATRES WITH ELBOW-RESTS

You can manipulate puppets in other ways, not just by holding your arms up in the air. Many inexperienced puppeteers find it hard to keep their arms held up for very long periods.

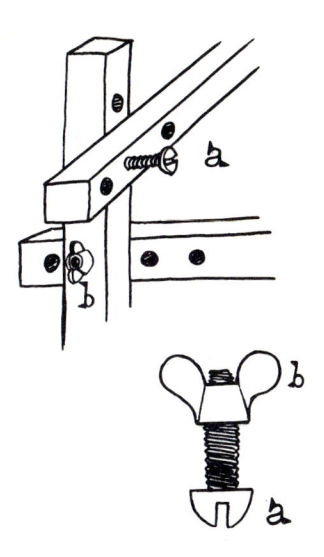

Lengths of wood of square section with holes bored in both directions can be used for home-made construction system.

A little elbow-rest theatre made of plywood. It can be put up on a table; here it is standing on two boxes with a board laid over them. The back curtain is divided in two so that the puppets can enter from the middle and both sides. (From 'Little Trine Trille and the Tigers', by Kirsten Ewaldsen and Benny E. Andersen.)

The theatre from the previous page seen from the front.

a elbow-rest; b ramp; c back-curtain.

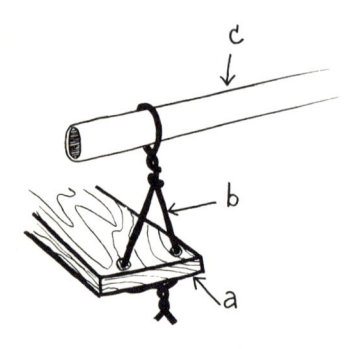

a elbow-rest; b wire; c side rod of the theatre.

They may prefer a puppet theatre with an elbow-rest – a board fitted inside the theatre a little below the playboard. You support your elbows on this rest while the puppets walk up and down. It follows that the manipulator must have a curtain in front of his face, so that the audience can't see him. Of course it can be very effective to show your face among the puppets now and again, but you should be able to hand over the stage entirely to them.

The back curtain in the scenery hangs down in front of the actor's face. Holes can be cut in the curtain and hidden with gauze or canvas painted the colour of the back curtain. You can look out through these holes at the audience and the puppets you are playing with.

In a theatre like this with elbow-rests you can play standing up or sitting down, but the movements of the puppets are seriously limited, and the performance may well give you backache, especially if you are sitting. Moreover you can easily get stuck fast in the kind of act the cuckoo-box theatre gives and so the method is not mentioned anywhere else in this book.

The closed theatre mentioned above can also be used as an elbow-rest theatre. A wooden board can be hung up with steel wire leading from the side rods and threaded through holes in the board. Since you can hang the curtains where you like in this kind of theatre it isn't difficult to hide the actor's face.

SCENERY THEATRE

You can build a theatre and put scenery into it, but you can also make a scene into a whole theatre! In Kjeld Iversen's comedy 'The Mysterious Parcel' there is a bus which is a whole puppet theatre – a scenery theatre.

The bus drives round the auditorium. That is, the wheels go round. You have to imagine the journey. The audience are present on the journey, and each time the bus stops you've come to a new place.

A theatre like this makes it possible to perform plays in new and surprising ways. The whole room is brought into the play and the audience are actually within the scenes.

On the other hand, you've got to build a whole new scenery theatre for the puppets if you feel you'd like to sail instead of drive. You cut a ship out of plywood and fit it firmly in a wooden trestle. A curtain cuts off the actors.

And then you have to build new scenery theatres for your puppets every time you want to change the scene.

The bus from 'The Mysterious Parcel'. The bus and the puppets were made by Jakob Mendel, Hanne Wilner Hansen and Kjeld Iversen (see also the drawing on page 84).

PUPPETS IN THE SCENERY THEATRE – AND LIGHT

In the scenery theatre, too, it is a good idea to sit on a little chair or a box with castors (see page 14). But you can also get up and walk round the room with your puppets quite openly, as we did in our first puppet plays. So long as we focus attention on the puppets we shan't destroy the illusion.

You need ordinary daylight or a ceiling light in the room, so that attention isn't drawn to a particular place, after all, the whole room is the scene. However, you may allow yourself a single photographic lamp trained on to the place in the scenery theatre where the puppets are actually performing.

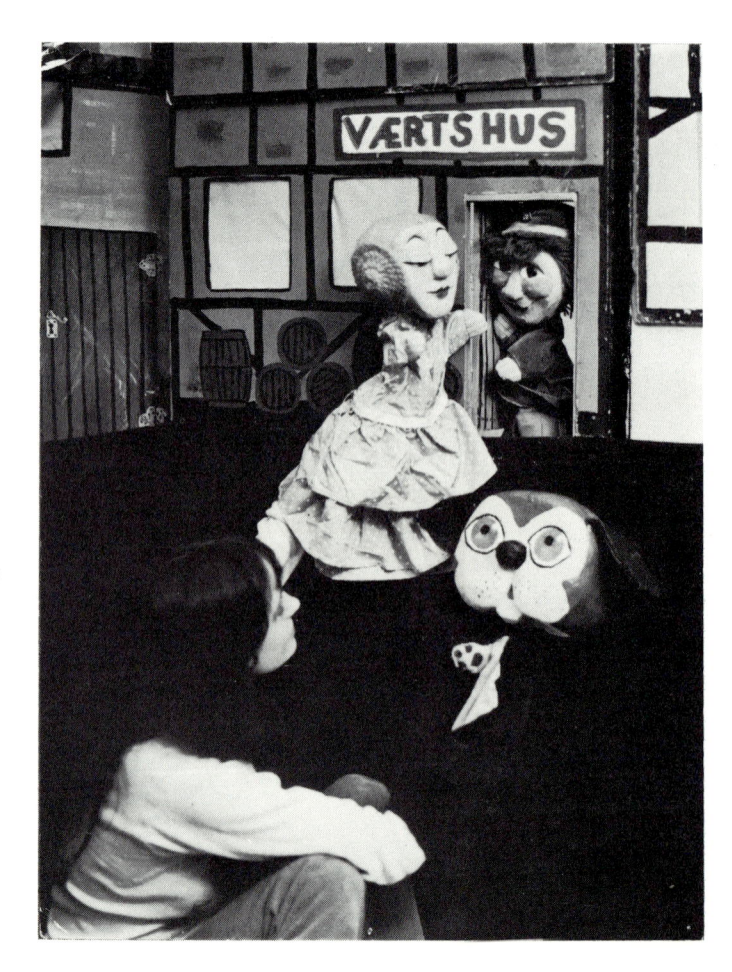

In the Comedy Wagon's puppet play adapted from Hans Andersen's fairy tale 'The Tinder-Box', the soldier goes round a town of houses which are all a kind of scenery theatre. They are cut out of plywood, and there are lights behind their windows covered with coloured plastic (bulbs in miniature sockets). The actors both work hidden behind the houses and openly among the audience.

82

When a puppet has to appear in a house, part of the house is lifted up and you can see into a room. (The puppet play was based on an idea by Carl Henrik Jensen, Trille and Benny E. Andersen. Scenery: Bo Bertram and Karsten Wolstad. Puppets: Bolette Bernild.)

If the prima donna prefers the closed cuckoo-box theatre, you can be pretty sure that her counterpart – the new puppet – will go for the scenery theatre. In the following play the two forms meet.

THE PRIMA DONNA'S SUCCESS

The bus is standing in the middle of the floor. The driver is sitting in it and driving. The closed theatre has its curtain drawn. The driver hoots with a little toy horn and waves to the audience.

'Hallo! Here I come driving my little bus. Honk honk! I've become a bus-driver. Shall we go for a ride?'

Various things happen on the journey (adapted from the play, 'The Mysterious Parcel'). There is a flower on the

PERFORMERS:
the prima donna
the new puppet as driver
the play-bus
the closed theatre
two actors
a gramophone
a record of operatic music

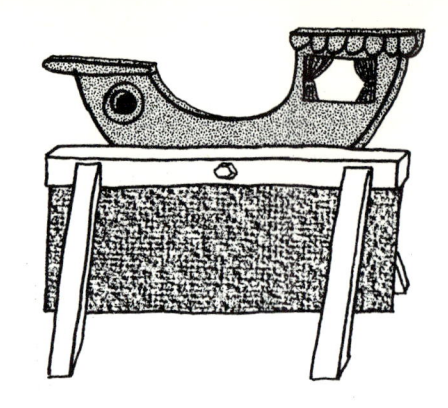

A simpler bus can be sawn out of plywood or cut out of strong cardboard. It must be big enough to conceal the actors, or it can be placed in front of a doorway with a curtain across it. Alternatively, it can be positioned like the ship illustrated above, which 'sails', fixed on top of a box.

bus's radiator which has to be watered with a little plastic watering can. There is an engine-imp under the bonnet, who can't be seen. He makes things go wrong with the engine and has to be caught before the bus will go. And then the driver has to get out of the bus and shove it. Meanwhile both driver and audience make motor-noises and cheer to get things going. At last everybody is pretty well out of breath. The bus stops, and the driver says:

'What's this I see? A real live theatre? We must have a look!'

The lights go up in the little puppet theatre and there is the pretty music of an overture from a gramophone.

The curtain rises on the prima donna standing in the middle of the stage. She flings out her arms and sings a beautiful aria, the music still coming from a gramophone record. When the item is finished she bows.

'Well, I must say,' says the driver, 'I am impressed. What a voice you have, and what an orchestra.'

The prima donna is pleased.

'Yes, haven't I? I've learned how it's done now. You don't have to say anything yourself. You can just use a gramophone or a tape recorder. The result will be much more impressive. And why should you use your voice when all the best singers and actors are available? I've had a tremendous success with this number. Terrific press notices and lots of money from the public. Thank you all so much. That's the end of this item.'

She bows again. The curtain falls and there is the sound of music, which gradually fades out.

The driver looks a bit startled. He looks first at the theatre and then at the audience.

'Well, yes. Everyone to his own taste. It sounds marvellous, but I'd rather sing myself. That's what I like best.'

He sings a pop song dreadfully out of tune. He may stop and say:

'But what does the audience like best? Oh, dash it! I'll get them to join in. Then they won't notice that I sing out of tune. Will you join in?'

If they say yes, he teaches them all a simple little tune to the following song. Or else he sings it by himself:

'I drive my little comic bus around
While others like a more dramatic sound.
You can't please everybody, that's well known,
So let them all get buses of their own.'

THE END

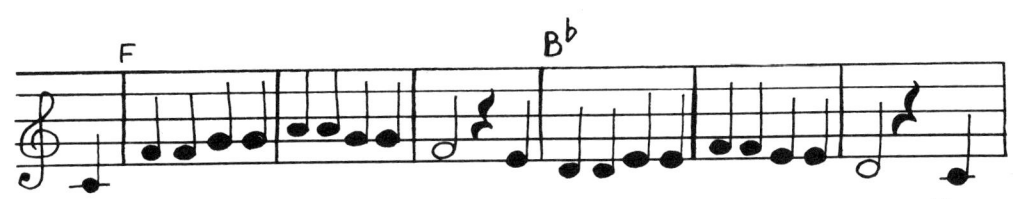

I drive my little comic bus around, While others like a more dramatic sound.   You can't please everybody, that's well known,   So let them all get buses of their own.

Postscript

SOME BOOKS ABOUT PUPPETS

Many books and articles have been written on the subject of the puppet theatre. You can get a list of them in the library, for example:
Philpott, A. R.: Modern Puppetry (London, 1966).

WARNING

If anyone comes along and tells you how the play ought to be produced to be 'correct', listen to this warning: no one knows. And the clever people who think they know all about it are generally the stupidest. Plays have made them look foolish for thousands of years and will go on doing so.

WHAT SHALL WE ACT?

There are also books of plays for the puppet theatre. They illustrate the kind of dialogue typical puppets use, and describe how these puppets are made.

You can also compose your own puppet plays. They can be written with lines that can be changed as you go along, or you can sketch them out by describing little situations, so that you only lay down the broad outline. Then the rest is improvised. Or you can play off the cuff and let the puppets decide where and how you're going. They will do it willingly, often with surprising results.

There are so many possibilities that it's a good thing to try out a lot of them. That's the only way you'll find out what you do best – at that moment. That's something that will change from day to day; the play never remains the same for long.

Where do you get what?

Some of the materials used in this book

Aluminium rods — For action rods on rod puppets.
See *Metal rods*.

Coloured bulbs — Shops that sell electrical equipment either have, or can obtain, coloured miniature bulbs up to 60 watts – for example, Osram.

Colour filters — For coloured lights, sold in sheets in many colours. Can be obtained from shops that deal in theatrical equipment.

Construction Frame — Easy to assemble.
For example: 'Speed Frame', marketed by Dexion Ltd, Slotted Angle Manufacturers, Maylands Avenue, Hemel Hempstead, Herts.

Cotton yarn — For puppets' wigs.
See *Knitting Wool*.

Doorhandle — – as a puppet.
Ironmongers will have various types in stock.

Expanded Polystyrene — Trade name Styrocell (U.K.), Styrofoam (U.S.A.). Used for puppets' heads. There are different hardnesses; the soft ones can be used for heads that are not intended for rough handling. Easy to cut. N.B. It will not withstand heat (it melts) and must be glued with synthetic resin glue. Can be bought from firms dealing with the materials for window decoration, insulation and packing. You may be able to get pieces from shops that deal in goods that are packed in these materials, such as radios and refrigerators.

Expanded Polystyrene balls	Can be used among other things for puppets' heads. Made in many sizes. Sold in shops dealing with articles for decoration; also by craft material stockists.
Gauze	For making puppets. Sold by the yard in shops that sell nursing supplies. Can also be obtained from chemists in the form of bandages. Buy tight-woven.
Glue	In the book we use Bostik or Uhu glue for gluing paper to cardboard or wood. Also for the puppets' wardrobe etc. Cellulose thinner is used to clean brushes. Synthetic resin glue, such as Evostick Resin 'W' or Vinylite is used for gauze mâché, gluing puppets' heads and for polystyrene. It can be thinned with water, which is also used for cleaning the brushes. Obtainable from stationers and suppliers of craft materials. Cellulose thinner and synthetic resin glue can also be bought from hardware shops.
Knitting wool, rug wool, or cotton yarn	For puppets' wigs. Can be bought in a wide variety of colours. Sold in wool shops and department stores.
Loofahs	For making puppets. From chemists and department stores.
Metal rods and wire	Rods for rod puppets – you can use, for example, brass or aluminium rods. Fencing wire is used for making spectacles, lorgnettes, etc. from ironmongers.
Net	Used for decorations. Can be bought from drapery shops.
Paints for puppets' heads	Matt paints sold in tubes by shops that sell artists' materials. See also *plastic paints*.
Piano castors	For the puppet manipulator's stool. Can be obtained or ordered from ironmongers.

Plasticine (modelling wax)   For making the models for puppets' heads.
Will generally be obtainable from artists' materials shops.
Sold in blocks, uncoloured.

Plastic paints

Suitable for the painting of decorations and puppets' heads. You can get the primary colours, red, blue and yellow, together with black and white, and mix them yourself. Acrylic or Polymer paints are suitable. Plastic paints are thinned with water and the brushes are also cleaned in water immediately after use.

Raffia

For puppets' wigs.
Can be obtained among other places at seed merchants, firms that deal in garden requirements, hardware shops, where it is also known as bast. Coloured raffia is obtained from craft material stockists.

Roller blinds

For shadow shows etc.
Can be bought from ironmongers and from firms that specialize in curtains and blinds.

Spring curtain rods

For use as puppets' arms.
Can be obtained from hardware shops among others. Curtain rods with brass fittings, which can be used for front curtains, and curtain rings for front curtains can also be bought from ironmongers and specialist shops.

Styrafoam/Styrocell   See *Expanded Polystyrene*

Trestles

For the scenery theatre, can be trestles for tables and washing trestles.
Can be bought from timber merchants.

Vilene

For 'ironing' decorations on net. Also called ironing Vilene.
Can be bought from drapery shops.

Useful tools to have

Brushes Brushes for painting the theatre, scenery, puppets' heads etc. Large brushes for coarse work, artists' brushes for fine work. Also pointed watercolour brushes for painting the details on the puppets' heads. Never let a brush stand on its bristles or hairs while drying or it will be ruined; rinse it and lay it on a table to dry.

Drill Metal drills can be obtained in plastic boxes in ten different sizes. Can also be used for wood.

File Metal file, not too coarse. Used for filing metal rods so that they don't scratch.

Fretsaw with blades Used among other things for making decorations out of plywood. There are several makes. Blades for metal can also be used for wood; they are stronger than the ordinary blades.

Hammer

Long needles Used for fastening puppets' clothes to their heads. Saddle-makers' needles can be used. You can also make them yourself out of knitting needles; the head is cut or sawn off and the end hammered flat, an eyehole is bored in the flat part and the side is filed.

Mechanical drill Not absolutely necessary, but it's useful to have one.

Pincers

Rubber hammer or wooden mallet More delicate than a metal hammer. Used for assembling the building set for puppet theatres.

Saw For woodwork – including the building of the theatre.

Screwclips Useful during the gluing process, while making puppets, for fixing scenery in the theatre and for many other things. You can get small screwclips which can be used for many purposes.

Screwdrivers In various sizes.

Shears, pliers and nippers Often come in useful.

Stanley knife Knife for cutting pasteboard and cardboard.